Table of Contents

BIOGRAPHY

Sitting on a wooden stool at three in the morning, placed in front of an illuminating screen is a man with the fire of the Holy Spirit burning from his mind and soul to his fingertips. This is more than dedication to a book, but the wisdom of the Lord Jesus Christ channeling down to a writer to enlighten us through this book. Glen Nichols is a writer that uses the Holy Scriptures to apply to our everyday life. People often feel as if the bible doesn't relate to today's issues; but this author proves that Gods heavenly wisdom is far better than man's earthly logic.

Born and raised in Cambridge Massachusetts, This is a man who seeks to use his God given gifts and talents to enhance the lives of others. Growing up in a Christian home, he was taught at an early age that service to others is what we all should be striving towards because this is where we find true satisfaction.

My Father has a profound sense of wisdom and grace that progresses his life. He is a wonderful Dad. He is a man of few words and great knowledge. He is something of a modern day Apostle. He loves to share his wisdom, knowledge and understanding to everyone through his writings. The words that you will read are coming from a man of a pure heart and utmost integrity. So read, ponder and digest these inspired words in this book because they will likely lead you to ''The pathway to faith''.

Ila G. Nichols

Authors Daughter

DEDICATION

This book is dedicated to the loving memory of my beloved mother Stella Nichols who went home to be with her Creator on January 2nd 2006. She left an indelible impression on all who knew her and had a special influence in the lives of all her children and grandchildren. She will be forever missed; and it is my hope that the effect of her legacy will influence the lives of all who endeavor to read through the pages of this book.

PREFACE

For most of us, all of our lives when we face hardships, we will hear people say things as keep the faith, hold onto your faith, don't lose faith or just have faith.

When I was growing up, one of the favorite songs at church was, "We've Come This Far by Faith." Somehow buried within the innate core of our souls, we understand that there is truth in these sayings and that faith is real. From time to time, we all hear or have heard the stories of the persons who with little to no resources and with the odds stacked insurmountably against them accomplish the miraculous. When we hear such stories, we are temporarily inspired to think that we can do the same. The good news is that we can. We all can. That inspired feeling that we get when we hear such stories is nothing but our measure of faith that is embedded in us being awakened from its slumber.

Faith needs to be constantly fed to remain awake and alert. If it is not consciously fed, it will inevitably return to its useless state of relaxation. The sad reality of this process is that every time that faith is allowed to return to its rest, its next stage of sleep becomes greater and more intense than the state before, hence, making it more difficult for us to accomplish those faith needing tasks that we are all called upon to carry out. This is the reason why as most people age, their achievements and exploits become lesser and lesser as opposed to becoming greater and greater. The Apostle Paul states in Romans 12:3, "That every man is given a measure of faith." The implication here is that a measure is something that can be added to or taken away from. When our faith is awakened, it marks OUR wake up call to keep adding to our given measure of faith by continuously feeding it and not letting it return to that useless state of rest. Everyone can do this. It is true that it will be more difficult for some than others because some have allowed this incredible giant of a servant (who does not understand the word impossible) to exists in the state of hibernation for most of their lives. For those people it might be a bit more difficult to awaken this great Goliath, but it can be done. Faith is a servant. Its desire and purpose is to serve you all of the days of your life but if you do not assign it tasks (whether they be great or small), it will lie in a state of dormancy.

The good news here is that when you make that conscious effort to activate your faith, you will begin to see that as your faith servant works for you and with you, others will be inspired, and this will awaken the faith giant in them; and it ignites a contagious positive cycle of inspiration that can only produce goodness in the creation of all human kind. The end result of this is that this pleases the Creator because He plainly states, "Without faith it is impossible to please me" (Heb. 11:6). Know that faith is real. Our spirit continually reveals it to us and it is true that with faith we can move mountains. Right now you may be walking in the dark valley of dismay concerning this wonderful virtuous gift given to us by our Creator; so come with me now on this exciting journey as we embark step by step to climb this mountain of faith, and as we begin to reach its pinnacle, you will begin to feel this prodigious companion awakening within you, and you will begin to see and understand just how faith really works.

This is the first volume of a five part series, the volumes will be comprehensive. Make sure that you acquire all five volumes and pass them onto friends and relatives.

Before we venture on this journey, I must emphasize that what you are about to read is not a personal philosophy. It is not an ideology concocted within the confines of my mind, nor is it a religious attempt to persuade individuals into something that could be true. What you are about to read is the result of over twenty years of research. This material is based on spiritual law, spiritual principle, and in many cases scientific facts. Before this book was written, I asked the Creator to guide my mind, heart, spirit, and hand as to the content that would be in this manuscript. Whenever any type of information is given, there must be some type of evidence or a reference that supports the content; otherwise, the information becomes an endless ramble of speculation. In this case, the ultimate reference that was used was the King James Version of the Holy Bible and the New King James Version for a clearer interpretation.

FOREWORD

Upon proof reading this manuscript, the principles of truth that emerged from its pages astonished me. In my opinion, the world would be a better place if everybody could grasp the timeless principles written all throughout this text. The author wonderfully illustrates universal truths in such a profound way so that any level of intellect can comprehend and understand the truth of what they are saying. I strongly believe that a book such as this should be mandatory reading in every institution of learning. This is a masterpiece. Without reservation, I highly recommend this book.

- Eugene Rivers D.D.

Eugene F. Rivers, the 3rd is an American activist, and Pentecostal minister based in Boston, Massachusetts.

He is the Pastor of the Azusa Christian Community, co-founder of the Boston Ten Point Coalition and co-chair of the National Ten Point Leadership Foundation. He has appeared on national television shows, including Hardball with Chris Matthews with Michael Rogers defending Rick Warren. He is also the special advisor to Bishop Charles Blake for Save Africa's Children.

CHAPTER ONE - *WHAT IS FAITH*

Just what is faith? Faith is a gift of substance given in measure to every man and woman from our Creator. Just as one would plant seeds into the substance of soil to receive a harvest, one must plant seeds in the form of thoughts, words, ideas and actions into the soil substance of faith to yield any return. Seeds come in many forms. In nature we have several types of seeds: apple seeds, pear seeds, peach seeds, apricot seeds, etc… Written in the DNA of every one of these seeds is the assignment to grow and reproduce after its likeness.

In the court that governs universal law, faith is the equivalent of substance & evidence; that same substance and evidence determines the end result of all things.

In the natural, after seeds are planted, we see a process take place. Those seeds must be first planted in fertile soil, they must be in the right environment, and they must be in the right geographical region in order to reproduce. We then see the seed has to die and sacrifice its life in order to give birth to the many generations of life that lie within that seed. If the seed refuses to die, it CANNOT REPRODUCE LIFE. Most people will read these words and accept this as truth because it is seen and proven every day in nature and in science. Many of these same people however will be reluctant to accept that this principle exists in the spirit realm. Let me say this, as it is in the spiritual, so it is in the natural. Hebrews 11:1 states, "Now faith is the SUBSTANCE of things hoped for, the EVIDENCE of things not seen."

Substance and evidence are the key words. In a court of law, during a trial, the key ingredients that are sought throughout the course of that trial are substance and evidence. <u>In the court that governs universal law, faith is the equivalent of substance & evidence; that same substance and evidence determines the end result of all things.</u>

The Creator himself used the law of faith to create the Earth. As stated before words are seeds and those seeds carry assignments. In Genesis chapter 1 we see how God the creator gave his words assignments to carry out their spoken tasks. Allow me to illustrate:

GENISIS CH.1

"*1* In the beginning God created the heaven and the earth.

2 And the earth was without form, and void; and darkness was upon the face of the deep. And the Spirit of God moved upon the face of the waters.

3 And God said, Let there be light: and there was light.

4 And God saw the light, that *it was good*: and God divided the light from the darkness.

5 And God called the light Day, and the darkness he called Night. And the evening and the morning were the first day.

6 And God said, Let there be a firmament in the midst of the waters, and let it divide the waters from the waters.

7 And God made the firmament, and divided the waters which *were* under the firmament from the waters which *were* above the firmament: and it was so.

8 And God called the firmament Heaven. And the evening and the morning were the second day.

9 And God said, Let the waters under the heaven be gathered together unto one place, and let the dry *land* appear: and it was so.

10 And God called the dry land Earth; and the gathering together of the waters called He Seas: and God saw that *it was* good.

11 And God said, Let the earth bring forth grass, the herb yielding seed, *and* the fruit tree yielding fruit after his kind, whose seed *is* in itself, upon the earth: and it was so.

12 And the earth brought forth grass, *and* herb yielding seed after his kind, and the tree yielding fruit, whose seed *was* in itself, after his kind: and God saw that it was good.

13 And the evening and the morning were the third day.

14 And God said, Let there be lights in the firmament of the heaven to divide the day from the night; and let them be for signs, and for seasons, and for days, and years:

15 And let them be for lights in the firmament of the heaven to give light upon the earth: and it was so.

16 And God made two great lights; the greater light to rule the day, and the lesser light to rule the night: *he made* the stars also.

17 And God set them in the firmament of the heaven to give light upon the earth,

18 And to rule over the day and over the night, and to divide the light from the darkness: and God saw that *it was* good.

19 And the evening and the morning were the fourth day.

20 And God said, Let the waters bring forth abundantly the moving creature that hath life, and fowl *that* may fly above the earth in the open firmament of heaven.

21 And God created great whales, and every living creature that moveth, which the waters brought forth abundantly, after their kind, and every winged fowl after his kind: and God saw that *it was* good.

22 And God blessed them, saying, Be fruitful, and multiply, and fill the waters in the seas, and let fowl multiply in the earth.

23 And the evening and the morning were the fifth day.

24 And God said, Let the earth bring forth the living creature after his kind, cattle, and creeping thing, and beast of the earth after his kind: and it was so.

25 And God made the beast of the earth after his kind, and cattle after their kind, and everything that creepeth upon the earth after his kind: and God saw that *it was* good.

26 And God said, Let us make man in our image, after our likeness: and let them have dominion over the fish of the sea, and over the fowl of the air, and over the cattle, and over all the earth, and over every creeping thing that creepeth upon the earth.

27 So God created man in his *own* image, in the image of God created he him; male and female created he them.

28 And God blessed them, and God said unto them, Be fruitful, and multiply, and replenish the earth, and subdue it: and have dominion over the fish of the sea, and over the fowl of the air, and over every living thing that moveth upon the earth.

29 And God said, Behold, I have given you every herb bearing seed, which *is* upon the face of all the earth, and every tree, in the which *is* the fruit of a tree yielding seed; to you it shall be for meat. *30* And to every beast of the earth, and to every fowl of the air, and to everything that creepeth upon the earth, wherein there is life, I have given every green herb for meat: and it was so.

31 And God saw everything that he had made, and, behold, *it was* very good. And the evening and the morning were the sixth day". KJV

As we can readily see in this illustration, God the Creator planted words into the soil substance of faith to create not only man, but all that exists. We see that all throughout this chapter, the method of faith unfolding before our eyes. In several verses throughout this chapter, if you read it closely, we see that it states, "God said.... And after He said, He saw..." This process has not stopped. Verse 27 tells us that we are created in his image **both male and female**. If we are created in His image, and He used words of faith to conceive creation, this means that we can use the same process to create things and circumstances in our own individual worlds.

If we reproduce this process of planting faith filled words into the soil substance of our lives, we will see these seeds begin to sprout just like a seed in the natural. The fruit of our words will produce and materialize in their season.

In Mark 11:22 - 24 Jesus Christ states this truth this way, *22* "Jesus answering saith unto them, Have faith in God.
23 For verily I say unto you, That whosoever shall say unto this mountain, Be thou removed, and be thou cast into the sea; and shall not doubt in his heart, but shall

believe that those things which he saith shall come to pass; he shall have whatsoever he saith.

24 Therefore I say unto you, What things soever ye desire, when ye pray, believe that ye receive *them*, and ye shall have *them*.

Many people will tell you that faith is just believing. What you just read negates the ideology that faith is only believing. Faith is not just believing, it is also speaking with your mouth the things that you desire and acting accordingly. It can be stated this way that saying, acting and believing will result in seeing.

If you will, allow me to borrow your imagination for a moment to illustrate faith in this light. Before I attempt to express this illustration you must understand this truth. It is a scientific fact that every object, substance and any form of matter vibrates. Rocks vibrate, people vibrate, books vibrate, cars vibrate, everything seen and unseen vibrates. Vibration runs through everything.

With that being said and established, let us proceed. As stated before, faith is a substance, (Hebrews 11:1) You are substance; the book that you have in your hands is a substance. Now here is where it gets interesting, the virtually invisible silk strand of web thread that a spider descends from the ceiling with is a substance as well. It is quite obvious that the spider's silk thread is a much finer and less dense substance than the book that you are holding in your hands right now. Here is what needs to be understood, what the spider's single silk thread is to the book, faith is to the spider's silk thread in reference to its density.

The density (vibration) of the book is probably 1 million times denser than that of the spiders strand and in the same way, the density (vibration) of the spiders strand is probably 100 million times denser than that of the substance of faith. Faith matter has no physical density that is why it cannot be seen. It is ethereal, **but it is just the same, A SUBSTANCE**. Remember what Hebrews 11:1 says, "Now faith is the **SUBSTANCE** of things hoped for, the **EVIDENCE** of things not seen." The more dense the substance (object), the heavier it becomes; and the less dense the substance (object) the lighter it becomes. Please keep in mind that all three are substances. The book is a paper substance, the single spider's strand is a silk substance, and faith itself is the ultimate substance that creates all things. One of them can be seen with the naked eye, one of them can be seen when a magnifying glass is applied, which confirms the evidence of its existence; and the other cannot be seen at all. Ironically, the substance matter of the one that cannot be seen is more real than the two that can be seen because it produced the two that can be seen. I will close with this illustration, If it were possible to reduce the vibration of faith to a much lower resolution, it would be only then that it would become a tangible substance that would be seen with the naked eye for the benefit of those who must see in order to believe.

> *When you understand how the faith process works, it becomes much easier to visualize and to manifest the things and circumstances that you want in your world.*

This invisible faith substance matter creates all living and tangible things. Once this truth is understood, you will see this is pure evidence of its living existence. Faith is a highly refined ethereal substance which originates in the spirit realm (the invisible world).

Let me paint a mental visual picture and break it down like this. Faith is like a physical substance that is so refined, that it is invisible. This same invisible substance of faith, is the definitive substance that creates everything, seen and unseen. In other words, everything that we see now, at one point was not seen and existed in the spirit realm. What birthed what we now see to its tangible state and into the earth realm (the visible world) was the invisible substance of faith. This faith substance is working all the time. This faith substance can create anything. When you understand how the faith process works, it becomes much easier to visualize and to manifest the things and circumstances that you want in your world. It is my prayer that this visual analogy of faith sheds light on its authenticity and greatly assists you in your endeavor to daily add to your God given measure.

This brings me to my next point; that being the acquisition of faith.

Romans 10:17 states, "…faith cometh by hearing…" Notice that it does not say that faith comes by seeing. People will tell you that seeing is believing….WRONG. The true statement to make here is that believing is seeing. Temporary faith comes from seeing, but permanent faith must come through the ear gate. If faith comes through hearing, this must mean that the inverse of this is true, that doubt and unbelief also comes by hearing. This should serve as a warning to us.

Words or "seeds" originating from the Creator are all pregnant with faith and are constantly pursuing the soil of receptive men's hearts. Words (faith filled or otherwise) that we allow to enter into our ear gate and germinate in the soil of our minds and hearts will carry out their spoken assignments. This behooves us as individuals to assign armed guardians to stand watch over our ear gates to ward off any rogue weeds from entering to choke the vulnerable dreams that are growing in the fertile pastures of our hearts and minds. King Solomon summed it up this way, "Keep your heart with all diligence; for out of it *are* the issues of life" (Proverbs 4:23).

Now we are beginning to see how we acquire faith. One of life's greatest tragedies is that most people live virtually faithless lives; they expend their lives having no idea why they were here. They were lost on the sea of life in an earthen vessel that was made after the likeness of its Creator with whom they tragically never made contact. Jesus Christ, the greatest master to ever teach life's principles, always taught that he gave us the keys to the Kingdom. The word Kingdom is key.

When one is a citizen of a kingdom, in principle, all of the responsibilities of the needs of the people of that kingdom lie squarely on the King's shoulders. It is the King's responsibility that every need (no matter how seemingly trivial) for every person within his kingdom is met. When the king (or Creator) placed you on this kingdom called Earth, he provided you (before you even arrived) with an assignment for your life and every one of your needs being met. Just as he wrote within the DNA of every fruit seed its assignment, He, the King and Creator, (Who loves you more than any human mind can fathom) wrote your life's assignment within your spirit. Jesus illustrated it as this "Are not five sparrows sold for two farthings and not one of them is forgotten before God? But even the very hairs of your head are all numbered. Fear not therefore; ye are of more value than many sparrows." (Luke 12: 6-7)

To put this all in its proper perspective, let me state this fact. Science proves that at the time of conception, every one of us was given special attention by an unseen force. When the male seed is dispersed in pursuit to impregnate the female egg, there are over four hundred thousand chances for us to be different individuals than who we are. Only one of those seeds had the correct script hand written (by the Creator) into its DNA which made you the individual that you are. Regardless of what you have been told in the past, you are a unique gift given to the world. There is an office for you to fill that is tailored and unique to your gifts, talents, and personality. This mandate lies within you and it is your job to locate it and to perform it. When you do this, you will find the fulfillment that you desperately seek.

I can almost hear you asking, "How do I find out what my assignment is?" This is my next point. Hebrews 11:6 states, "But without faith, *it is* impossible to please *him*, for he that cometh to God (the Creator) must believe that he is, and that he is a rewarder of those *that* diligently seek him." Here is your answer. He made the first move by creating you. Now, it's your move. I must stress however, the key word here is diligence. You must diligently seek and ask the Creator to show you your assignment. If you must fast, (put aside food for a while until you receive your answer) it is worth every hunger pang and then some. When you diligently seek him, He will answer you and He will reward you by revealing to you your assignment. It may happen through a dream or through different circumstances, but you will know.

When you receive the answer, ask then for the confirmation. Upon receiving your confirmation, you will begin to see how people will begin to come into your life at the right time and that circumstances will seem to just fall into place. This is the way that it is supposed to be. This happens to all individuals that have "found their way." It is the most wonderful feeling in the world. This is the plan that the Creator devised for each human, but only a disconcerting few ever get to experience this. For those readers who have children, if you would, look at it like this; in a sense, you and your spouse created that child and nothing thrills a parent more to know that their children have found their way in life. How much more is this true of the loving Creator of mankind? It pleases Him when His children find and are fulfilling their assignments. His desire is that all of His children live out their assignments and through this process; they will bring life and blessings to themselves and many others in this life.

CHAPTER TWO – *WORDS ARE FAITH SEEDS*

In the Old Testament, all of the Jewish patriarchs blessed their sons and the children of Israel with the "spoken blessing;" And consequently the Jewish people are the most blessed people on this earth. This proves the power of words. Words are seeds and seeds carry assignments. I cannot stress this point enough. You can bless and curse people just with words; James 3:10 states, "Out of the same mouth proceeds blessing and cursing. My brethren, these things ought not so to be."

> *Children should always be told the truth, because the truth liberates and frees one from bondage.*

As a child growing up, I remember a famous neighborhood saying, "Sticks and stones can break my bones but names will never hurt." Children are taught such sayings as defense mechanisms to help pacify the offensive and painful experiences that the adolescent years can bring. Out of ignorance, parents still to this day teach children such sayings thinking they are protecting their children from these painful encounters. The reality here is, they are doing more harm than good to their children. <u>Children should always be told the truth, because the truth liberates and frees one from bondage.</u> Parents should always tell their children the truth.

When words in the form of destructive forces are spoken to a child, that child should be instructed to speak back to the source with positive words of affirmation that will negate and nullify the negative words just spoken to him or her. What does this do? This will put up a protective wall of resistance and will weaken any future destructive attacks coming from that same source. This will also help to propel the mental and emotional maturity needed to protect and develop the person on the inside of them.

King Solomon says in Proverbs 18: 21, "Death and life are in the power of the tongue: and they that love it shall eat the fruit thereof." Words are more than just mere things that have no consequences. This is proven every day in court rooms. The wrong thing is said out of impatience or anger resulting in unfavorable circumstances for many individuals.

If parents only knew the creative and destructive value of words, they would be much more careful of what they say to their children and what they allow their children to hear. Words can have eternal consequences. Generations of families have been cursed and blessed because of words spoken. Marriages and divorces happen because of words. Children are born because of words. Wars are started because of words. Wars are ended because of words. People are murdered because of words. Revenge is executed because of words. Gifts are given because of words. Inheritances are lavishly bestowed upon individuals because of words. Wealth is created because of words. I hope that by now you are beginning to see and understand that words are very potent seeds.

The words that you speak are seeds that are cast into the heart and mind soil of the individuals hearing them. Weather you believe it or not, every word that is spoken is being recorded; and we all will give an account for our words and deeds in this life. Listen to what Jesus said in Matthew 12:36, "BUT I SAY UNTO YOU, THAT EVERY IDLE WORD THAT MEN SHALL SPEAK, THEY SHALL GIVE ACCOUNT THEREOF IN THE DAY OF JUDGEMENT." The words that we speak should be faith filled words. Faith filled words are seeds that accomplish positive things when they sprout and reach their full term.

When we as parents speak to our children, we should speak to them words of positive affirmation. More often than not when children do not measure up to the standards of parents, parents often make the fatal mistake of telling their children that they will never amount to anything. This is one of the worst things that you can tell a child. I cannot emphasize this enough. WORDS ARE SEEDS AND HUMAN HEARTS AND MINDS ARE FERTILE SOIL. The younger the person, the more impressionable and fertile the soil tends to be. This young fertile soil is given to you on loan for roughly eighteen years. **Your job as a farmer is to tend to that fertile acreage and to plant vegetation in the form of**

WORDS & IDEAS, which will help to produce thoughts, which must be fertilized by that child's actions. The ultimate purpose of this process is so the fruit of your labor will yield a nourishing harvest for the purpose and for the good of all mankind for many generations to come.

Just as there are faith filled words that go forth and plant faith and prosperity, there are also words of doubt when they go forth, they plant despair and destruction. This is the unfortunate case of most of the words that come out of the mouths of people the world over. If your desire is to be successful in your life's work, it is imperative, that you steer clear of all those who speak constant words of doubt. These people may be well meaning in their purpose for telling you the things that they do. Often times these people are close relatives which makes it hard on those of us who have an understanding of the detrimental consequences that these associations can mean to our success.

These individuals who speak these words of doubt have no idea of the damage that they can cause. If you are wise, you would limit your time around them. The best thing that you can do for these people is to fulfill your life purpose; in doing that, you show them and others through your actions and accomplishments that your method is the correct method. Your level of success will give you a platform from which you can speak to them and others and you will be able to teach and enlighten them to the ways of wisdom.

To help sum this up and to illustrate the power of words as faith seeds, the listen to what the greatest master, Jesus Christ, teaches about spiritual law and the way that words act as seeds

Matthew 13:1-23

"*1* The same day went Jesus out of the house, and sat by the sea side.

2 And great multitudes were gathered together unto him, so that he went into a ship, and sat; and the whole multitude stood on the shore.

3 And he spake many things unto them in parables, saying, Behold, a sower went forth to sow;

4 And when he sowed, some *seeds* fell by the way side, and the fowls came and devoured them up:

5 Some fell upon stony places, where they had not much earth: and forthwith they sprung up, because they had no deepness of earth:

6 And when the sun was up, they were scorched; and because they had no root, they withered away.

7 And some fell among thorns; and the thorns sprung up, and choked them:

8 But other fell into good ground, and brought forth fruit, some an hundredfold, some sixtyfold, some thirtyfold.

9 Who hath ears to hear, let him hear.

10 And the disciples came, and said unto him, Why speakest thou unto them in parables?

11 He answered and said unto them, Because it is given unto you to know the mysteries of the kingdom of heaven, but to them it is not given.

12 For whosoever hath, to him shall be given, and he shall have more abundance: but whosoever hath not, from him shall be taken away even that he hath.

13 Therefore speak I to them in parables: because they seeing see not; and hearing they hear not, neither do they understand.

14 And in them is fulfilled the prophecy of Isaiah, which saith, By hearing ye shall hear, and shall not understand; and seeing ye shall see, and shall not perceive:

15 For this people's heart is waxed gross, and *their* ears are dull of hearing, and their eyes they have closed; lest at any time they should see with *their* eyes, and hear with their ears, and should understand with *their* heart, and should be converted, and I should heal them.

16 But blessed *are* your eyes, for they see: and your ears, for they hear.

17 For verily I say unto you, That many prophets and righteous *men* have desired to see *those things* which ye see, and have not seen *them*; and to hear *those things* which ye hear, and have not heard *them*.

18 Hear ye therefore the parable of the sower.

19 When any one heareth the word of the kingdom, and understandeth *it* not, then cometh the wicked *one*, and catcheth away that which was sown in his heart. This is he which received seed by the way side.

20 But he that received the seed into stony places, the same is he that heareth the word, and anon with joy receiveth it;
21 Yet hath he not root in himself, but dureth for a while: for when tribulation or persecution ariseth because of the word, by and by he is offended.
22 He also that received seed among the thorns is he that heareth the word; and the care of this world, and the deceitfulness of riches, choke the word, and he becometh unfruitful.
23 But he that received seed into the good ground is he that heareth the word, and understandeth it; which also beareth fruit, and bringeth forth, some an hundredfold, some sixty, some thirty" KJV.

Remember that faith filled words will always sprout and produce a harvest. We humans are God's highest form of creation. We are made in his likeness. We are the only creatures from His creation that was blessed with the gift of speech which allows us to create with our words. We inherited this creative ability in the process of our formation. It is most unfortunate that most people are unaware of this truth; and as a result, most people just exist from day to day and never use this creative power. It is my hope that by reading this book that you will begin to see and understand the creative power of words and start to walk in your destiny.

When the Creator created the Earth, He did not do it using physical material goods. He did it with words of faith. King Solomon said, "**Death and life are in the power of the tongue: and they that love it shall eat the fruit thereof" (Proverbs 18:21)**. Words can be creative or destructive forces. Words are extremely powerful things. Please be careful how you use them.

CHAPTER THREE - *KEEPING FAITH AWAKE*

Just how does one keep faith in its awakened state? Every day we allow many thoughts to pass through and infiltrate our minds. Every thought that we think carries energy with it. The energy that each thought carries is either that of strength (faith) or weakness (fear). Here is the litmus test. When we are given great news, like a healthy child being born into the family, a job promotion, a great accomplishment of a child, a marriage proposal etc... This makes us feel great and we allow our minds to dwell on those thoughts as we rightfully should. The more that we think of this good news, the more energetic we feel, the stronger we feel, and the <u>healthier we feel</u>. These thoughts of strength give us energy and power.

> *Most individuals never stop and think that their moods, feelings, attitude, posture, finances, and health are controlled by their thoughts. This is why it is imperative that we keep our minds pregnant with thoughts of faith.*

Now let's view the flip side of this truth. When we hear that a close love one has just died, or we hear an unfavorable medical prognosis, or that a child is terminally ill, etc... Most of us will slump into a temporary state of depression and we then experience feelings of sadness, despair and melancholy. Most people never stop and think that their moods, feelings, attitude, posture, finances and health, are controlled by their thoughts. Some will read this and the light will come on. This needs to be emphasized. If you would, please stop reading this book and take two minutes to ponder this statement. I will repeat it again.

Most individuals never stop and think that their moods, feelings, attitude, posture, finances, and health are controlled by their thoughts. This is why it is imperative that we keep our hearts and minds pregnant with thoughts of faith.

Paul, the apostle summed it up this way "Finally my brethren, whatsoever things are true, whatsoever things *are* honest, whatsoever things *are* just, what so ever things *are* pure, whatsoever things *are* lovely, whatsoever things *are* of a good report, if *there be* any virtue, if *there be* any praise, THINK ON THESE THINGS." (Phillipians 4:8) I cannot go on without pointing out these attributes that he suggests that we meditate on, things that are true, honest, just, pure and lovely. He advises us to think about things that are of a good report; virtuous things, and things that are praiseworthy.

I can almost hear some readers saying that this sounds very idealistic; and I concur to a great degree that it is. Let's put it in these terms. Everything good that has ever been created started with an idealistic thought. The beautiful house you live in, the great career that you have, you're beautiful spouse, your family, the nice car you drive etc... All started by having idealistic thoughts. Children live with ideal thoughts, they can teach us a great deal about idealistic thinking and they can teach us a great deal about faith. It is no wonder the master, Jesus Christ, said "Suffer little children, and forbid them not, to come unto me: for such is the kingdom of heaven." Matt.19:14. In order to enter the kingdom, we must become like a child. Child-like faith is something that should increase as we grow into adulthood but unfortunately in most instances, this is not the case. Children should be taught in the ways of faith early on in life. They should always be encouraged to feed their faith and to keep it awake. The problem is that parents themselves fail to understand that they themselves were given a measure of faith that daily needs to be added to. That's why manuscripts such as this and others with like content should be read many times over and digested for the purpose assisting in one's spiritual development.

> *At birth every child is given an internal sterling goblet. This goblet is filled to the brim by our creator with a precious golden spiritual liquid called faith or better said "childlike faith".*

Have you ever noticed that when you tell a child that they can become anything in life that they want to become that they believe you? As a child, I can remember my beloved and saintly late mother stating these very words to me on numerous occasions and every time she would utter those words to me, I can vividly remember an excitement welling up on the inside of me and making me feel like the sky was the limit as to what I could achieve in this life. I now understand as an adult what was happening. What she was doing was adding to my measure of childlike faith. Remember that faith comes by hearing. (Romans 10:17)

Allow me if you would to illustrate it this way. At birth every child is given an internal sterling goblet. This internal goblet is filled to the brim by our creator with a precious golden spiritual liquid called faith or better said "childlike faith". "This is your given measure of faith" (Romans 12:3). This golden liquid is the internal spiritual fuel that we will need throughout the course of our lives to carry out our life's work, to aid us in attaining our dreams, and it will be needed for us to accomplish those things that we are called upon to achieve. The external storms and pressures of life come to internally shake and test us; and in the process they will inevitably; spill to the ground a portion of our precious given measure of liquid faith. Every time that we are tested in this way it represents an opportunity to replace that spilled portion of faith with a little bit more than what was lost with that experience. Peter illustrates this truth like this. "...The trial of your faith, being more precious than gold that perisheth, though it be tried with fire might be found unto praise and honor at glory at the appearing of Jesus Christ" (1Peter 1:7).

Most people do not understand that this is what happens when adverse circumstances befall them. It is nothing more than an opportunity in disguise to help propel them into their life's assignment and to equip them with the faith and patience (faith is not gained overnight) needed for their success. The Epistle James puts it this way, "Knowing this, that the trying of your faith worketh patience" (James 1:3).

Have you ever noticed those who are the high achievers in this life usually had to overcome the most? It is the person who adds to their measure of faith (whether they do it consciously or unconsciously) that will achieve. It is our duty as individuals that as we grow to keep that liquid faith in that goblet as close to the brim as possible. That is why it is extremely important if you have young children that your steer them in the ways of faith at an early age.

It is your job as a parent to find out what gifts and talents dwell on the inside of your child. Is it a scientist that is inside? Is it a doctor? Is it an athlete? Is it a lawyer, a writer, etc…King Solomon states it this way, "Train up a child in the way he should go: and when he is old, he will not depart from it" (Proverbs 22:6). Allow me to put what he is saying here in today's vernacular. Solomon (The wisest king to ever reign) (1 Kings 3:10-13) is instructing us to bring up our children according to the God given gifts and talents that were placed in them at birth. He is telling us to point each individual child in the direction that they are destined to go in. They may stray away from the path, but if they were exposed to the right path early on they will return to it later in life.

> *Speak only positive affirmations to that child, nurture those positive seeds of confirmation and watch, observe and be blessed as the genius unfolds!*

A very helpful indication of perceiving the intrinsic God given gifts your children possess is by finding out what they naturally take a liking to and what they naturally do well at. Throughout this process, do not forget to always ask the Creator to show you who your child is. When you find out what that gift or those gifts (some children have multiple gifts and talents) are, always build up their faith concerning them and encourage them to pursue a career in those areas. <u>Speak only positive affirmations to that child, nurture those positive seeds of confirmation and watch, observe and be blessed as the genius unfolds!</u>

If I had my way, every child in the world would have the following instilled in them from early on; and if this were the case, every elementary school student around the world would possess the following knowledge. They would be told that when they were born they were given a very big strong invisible man to help them on this journey called life; his name is FAITH. He is your link and your connection to your Creator. The reason why he was given to you is to keep you in continuous contact with your Creator. He is extremely powerful. He is so strong that he can pick up a mountain and throw it HUNDREDS of miles into the sea. When you grow up you will learn that mountains really do sit at the bottom of the ocean. He is your friend. He was given to you by your Creator. He is invisible, but the works he performs are very visible. He is your servant and you can make him do anything your heart desires. Every time you give him a command, he becomes stronger and more powerful. He is as Superman, but instead of kryptonite making him weak your doubt and your unbelief will make him weak and render him helpless. When he becomes helpless he falls asleep. It is your job to never let him go to sleep. He hates to sleep. Your job is to EXERCISE HIM by giving him tasks and jobs to do and keep him active every day of your life. Just as Hercules was given Pegasus as a gift at birth, in the same way did your Creator give you your giant faith companion as a gift at birth. The only difference is that this is not a myth; this is as real as it gets.

Many people will try to tell you that he does not exist, but DON'T YOU BELIEVE THEM. One of the reasons why people will tell you that he does not exist is because they were never told that he was given to them at birth. Refrain from staying around those people too long. If you ever find yourself doubting that he is there, just go back and remember some of the jobs that you gave him to do in the past and your belief will immediately come back to you.

Every morning when you wake up and every night before your go to sleep, thank your Creator for this wonderful gift named faith that he has given you. Always remind yourself of the wonderful things that he has brought to you in the past. You must always be grateful to your Creator for this wonderful gift. Many people will see the things that you accomplish and will be attracted to you as you travel on your journey. Your job is to tell them that they too were given this companion at birth and that he needs to be awakened and kept active and exercised in their lives as well.

As you grow older, you will find greater and greater things you will be called on to do. YOU MUST NEVER FORGET THAT YOUR GIANT FRIEND DOES NOT KNOW THE WORD IMPOSSIBLE. HE

CAN DO ANYTHING. He is your direct connection to the one that created everything. Without your faith companion you will never be able to please your Creator. The more that you commune with your faith friend; he will begin to tell you what your purpose for being on this Earth is. When you finally know your purpose, you are to pursue it and work at it with everything in you. You must never let anybody drive you away from that purpose. This is the job that was made for you and only you can do it the way that it is supposed to be done.

When you perform your life's work, your service to your fellow man will help and benefit many people. As you act upon your calling, you will inspire countless others to discover their life's work. Due to your obedience you will be greatly rewarded in this life and in the life to come when you leave this Earth.

Because of a child's impressionable mind, he or she will believe this truth and when these seeds of faith take root, they will remain intact and grow with that child into their adult years. Children who are given this proper spiritual attention are destined for nothing less than greatness.

What if these seeds were planted, fertilized, and nurtured in every child that is now growing up around the world. If this were the case, one could only imagine the world that the following generation of adults would live in.

CHAPTER FOUR - *UNDERSTANDING FAITH*

I am of the reminded of the time that I visited a Pentecostal church in Waipahu, Hawaii. The minister was telling the congregation of his early years in the ministry. He stated when he started out in the ministry he would frequently receive many invitations to preach on the mainland (United States). He, being a young clergyman, was eager to jump at these opportunities to fly abroad and help spread the Gospel. Several of the invitations that he accepted however, would not be accompanied with an airline ticket.

When he would call back to the parties that sent the invitation, he would tell them they forgot to include the flight accommodations. The inviting party on several occasions would respond saying, "Brother, can't you come by faith?" He would then wittingly and sarcastically respond saying, "I have looked in the phone book several times in the past for 'Faith Airlines' and I never found it; so for that reason, I can't come by faith."

This true story, as humorous as it is, represents somewhat of a barometer of how many "people of faith" truly misunderstand the whole notion of faith. I have found in my experience that most "faith people" do not really have their full understanding completely wrapped around this faith concept. Before we delve into understanding what faith is, let us take a back door approach. Let us look at what faith is not; let us look at the antonym of faith. Most people know the opposite of faith is fear. My mother had a saying when I was a child, "When fear comes knocking at the door, send faith to answer it."

> *It has been said that Mike Tyson, former Heavyweight Boxing Champion of the world, used the art of fear and intimidation on his opponents to defeat them prior to the bout;*

Throughout history, greater armies have lost wars to lesser armies because the greater army had succumbed to fear. It has been said that Mike Tyson, former Heavyweight Boxing Champion of the world, used the art of fear and intimidation on his opponents to defeat them prior to the bout; so before the bell even sounded, fear had already taken root and many of his opponents were already defeated in their own minds.

Because of fear, books are not written, marriages are not pursued, buildings are not built, and careers are not sought after. Fear brings sickness, failure, ridicule, and always has a damaging effect. When fear is present, failure will be always lurking in the shadows. Fear is the common thread interwoven throughout the fabric of every form of failure. It is most terrible and those that are seeking success should never embrace it. Ironically enough, as destructive as fear is, it is very much a needed motivating nemesis for those that are seeking success along the pathway of life. Fear should only be used as a motivating force to keep a person on the path of success. Just as how the negative emotion of anger creates an energy that can be used and directed in a positive way; so should fear be used in a similar fashion; to steer one clear from the ravages of failure and destruction. Remember, fear is meant to be an external motivator; never an internal motivator. Fear was never meant to be consumed. When fear is internalized, it is like an ocean going vessel taking on water. Once the air cavity is full with water, the vessel will sink. When a person allows fear to rent cerebral space, it will spread like an uncontrollable wildfire. If you ever find yourself in this type of situation, make sure that you immediately extinguish that destructive fire.

The personal remedy that I use when I find that fear tries to overtake my thoughts; is that I repeat Psalms 27 out loud as many times as need until faith returns. Listen to these words of faith as I quote them; listen to how these words dispel the negative emotion of fear.

PSALMS CH. 27

"*1* The Lord *is* my light and my salvation; whom then shall I fear? The Lord *is* the strength of my life; of whom shall I be afraid?

2 When the wicked, *even* my enemies and my foes, came upon me to eat up my flesh, they stumbled and fell.

3 Though an host should encamp against me, my heart shall not fear: though war should rise against me, in this *will* I *be* confident.

4 One *thing* have I desired of the Lord, that will I seek after; that I may dwell in the house of the Lord all the days of my life, to behold the beauty of the Lord, and to inquire in his temple.

5 For in the time of trouble he shall hide me in his pavilion: in the secret of his tabernacle shall he hide me; he shall set me up upon a rock.

6 And now shall mine head be lifted up above mine enemies round about me: therefore will I offer in his tabernacle sacrifices of joy; I will sing, yea, I will sing praises unto the Lord.

7 Hear, O Lord *when* I cry with my voice: have mercy also upon me, and answer me.

8 *When thou saidst,* Seek ye my face; my heart said unto thee, Thy face, Lord, will I seek.

9 Hide not thy face *far* from me; put not thy servant away in anger: thou hast been my help; leave me not, neither forsake me, O God of my salvation,

10 When my father and my mother forsake me, then the Lord will take me up.

11 Teach me thy way, O Lord, and lead me in the plain path, because of mine enemies.

12 Deliver me not over unto the will of mine enemies: for false witnesses are risen up against me, and such as breathe out cruelty.

13 *I had fainted,* unless I had believed to see the goodness of the Lord in the land of the living.

14 Wait on the Lord: be of good courage, and he shall strengthen thine heart: wait, I say, on the Lord" KJV.

PSALMS CH.23

Another fear busting Psalm is Psalm 23, "*1* The Lord *is* my shepherd; I shall not want.
2 He maketh me to lie down in green pastures: he leadeth me beside the still waters.
3 He restoreth my soul: he leadeth me in the paths of righteousness for his name's sake.
4 Yea, though I walk through the valley of the shadow of death, I will fear no evil: for thou art with me; thy rod and thy staff they comfort me,
5 Thou preparest a table before me in the presence of mine enemies: thou anointest my head with oil; my cup runneth over.
6 Surely goodness and mercy shall follow me all the days of my life: and I will dwell in the house of the Lord for ever" KJV.

The next time you feel overtaken with fear, find the nearest bible, turn to one of these two chapters, meditate on the words and watch what happens.

Another teaching that misleads many astray in the area of faith is something called blind faith. Just what is blind faith? Blind faith is in short making up one's own rules about faith. Blind faith is attempting to do things in ignorance and believing that if you believe something to be true, then it becomes true for you. If you believe it not to be true, then it is not true for you.

Let me emphasize this one point, FAITH IS A LAW whether we believe it or not. All universal laws are established, complete, and orderly. One must operate within the confines of these laws in order to get predictable desired results. Let me clarify this. A person might not believe in the law of gravity; so to defy the law and to prove that it is not true for them, they proceed to jump off of a building and expect to float slowly to the Earth. This person going on blind faith is going to find out in short order the very painful experience that **law is the truth, and truth is the law**. It does not matter if we believe the truth or not it shall always remain constant. Universal laws were working before we got here, they are working at this very moment, and they will be working long after we are gone.

Whenever a person is in violation of any law, punishment will be imminent. Blind faith can be extremely dangerous because it defies universal law. This will ultimately result in failure, and failure automatically sends a V.I.P invitation to the twins of devastation, doubt and fear. This tandem, if allowed to rent mind space will destroy any dream. If you have been operating in blind faith and you find you self being overwhelmed by doubt and fear, remember that the antidote for these brothers of destruction are Faith and hope. **Faith and hope are the arch rivals of doubt and fear. When faith and hope are invited back into that same cerebral space, they will null and void any**

tenancy lease that was endorsed by the former destructive tenants.

Now that we understand what faith is not, let us take a look at understanding what faith is. Before I continue here, I could write the next five hundred pages on explaining what faith is, but for the sake of time and space we will only focus on the areas that are pertinent to getting results. As stated earlier, faith is a law or if you will, a principle. When one speaks of a law or principle, this means that certain regulations must be followed in order for things to properly flow.

According to Webster's American dictionary the definition of a law is as follows: LAW equals "A principle based on predictable consequences of an act; condition etc... the law of supply and demand, a commandment or a revelation from God, a mathematical rule."

What I hear in these definitions and the word that rings in my head when I read them is the word ACCURACY. It is safe to say that applied law or principle equals accuracy. Faith is a law. It is a law that originated in the spirit realm. Just as natural laws carry conditions, spiritual laws carry conditions as well. Let us take for example a law that everybody understands the law of planting and harvesting. We all understand that if and when the farmer puts seeds in the ground, in time, he will receive crops. We do not see the process what happens inside of the soil, because we cannot see beneath the ground. We do understand however, that the farmer has to operate within the confines of this law by planting, tending to, and fertilizing those seeds in order for the law to go into effect. Predictable results are always contingent on these conditions being met.

As in any other field of study it will take a little time to learn the conditions of the law of faith. I often equate spiritual laws to geometrical laws. When one firsts studies geometry, they often think that they are applying the proper geometrical principles to the given equation. When they discover that they are unsuccessful in finding the correct answers, they often get discouraged and conclude that the principles do not work. When they are shown however, that they either did not correctly apply the principles or that they are missing an application or two, they soon see that the principle is law; and that the problem did not lie in the principle, but that the problem lied in their application of the principle.

The same theory that applies with geometrical principles applies with all spiritual law. When correctly applied the law CANNOT FAIL. There is NEVER an exception to the rule. It works 100% of the time when correctly applied. These laws are as new as they are old; and it is always exciting to see the inevitable results when we apply them to our lives.

CHAPTER FIVE - *FAITH AND LOVE*

Faith and love act as two of the fingers on the hand of God. They work in unison; inwardly fashioning and perfecting all of those who are willing to become light beacons to illuminate the pathway of life to a dark and fallen world. Faith and love work harmoniously. It is love however, that is the greater of the two. 1 Corinthians 13:13 states, "And now abideth faith, hope, and love, these three but the greatest of these *is* love."

> *What water is to the maintenance of physical health, love is to the sustenance of emotional health.*

Love, like water is essential for life to exist. We were all born of water (John 3:5) and need water to sustain natural health; what water is to the maintenance of physical health, love is to the sustenance of emotional health. We need to be taught what love is. Every man and living organism constantly seeks love. The reason for this is because all living things were created from the very essence of love itself. The sad reality is that few truly understand the method of "real" love.

We have all heard that statement that "there is a thin line between love and hate." This is the biggest misnomer concerning "true" love that I have ever heard.

This statement is extremely accurate; however, when it comes to the selfish love or "lust" that originates from the flesh, the chasm between "true" love and hate is the same distance between heaven and hell.

When most of us think of love we usually think about the love between a man and a woman. Let's take a close look at this.

When God the Creator created mankind, he was in an innocent and glorified state. When sin entered into the world through disobedience, mankind lost his innocence and the glory that encircled him departed. God our Creator provided through his Son Jesus Christ provision for us to be redeemed back into fellowship with himself; and through this process retrieve a renewed spirit. Ephesians 4: 22-24 states, "*22* That ye put off concerning the former conversation the old man, which is corrupt according to the deceitful lusts;
23 And be renewed in the spirit of your mind;
24 And that ye put on the new man, which after God is created in righteousness and true holiness" KJV.

If I were a marriage counselor, I would insist that every couple that came through my door for counseling memorize these three verses. God the creator purposed for man to originate love and to give love from his spirit. When this method is followed, everything falls in line. What am I saying? Within us all, our flesh and spirit are constantly in an endless battle. Whichever one we accommodate will become the dominant and will take precedence over our actions. If I can put it to you this way, we all have two dogs that live inside of us. One is a flesh dog, and the other one is a spirit dog. Whichever one we feed the most will grow stronger and will overtake the other and consequently we will cater to that area of our makeup.

The whole crux of the message of this book is designed to speak to, and to motivate your spirit man. If or when I do that, my goal will be accomplished.

We have all seen the cartoons where a person is trying to make a decision and the little angel and the little demon are on either shoulder whispering to the individual to make up their mind. To a certain degree that is true. The angel in this case would appeal to the spirit of that person, and the demon appeal to their flesh.

Every living person is a soul that has a spirit that lives in a body, hence, the makeup of a man: body, soul and spirit.

When people get married, what happens is that they become one flesh (Matthew 19:5). Before I elaborate any further, let us look at Ephesians 4:23 one more time, "And be renewed in the spirit of your mind;" In case you are unaware of it, your spirit looks just as you. It has your two eyes, your two arms, your two legs, all of your features etc... It is you in spirit form. When you die it will rise up out of your body and go into the next life. That spirit body also has a mind. Verse 23 tells us to be renewed in the spirit of your mind or it can be said this way, be renewed in your spirits mind. This is the spawning ground where the love for your spouse is meant to originate. If your spirit mind is renewed than your natural mind will also be renewed. The love that originates from the renewed spirit mind is a Christ like love. It is a love that looks to give and not take. The renewed spirit mind enters into the marriage relationship seeking to improve your spouse's life in any and every way.

On the contrary, the love (or lust) that that originates out of the fleshly or the natural mind enters into the marriage relationship looking for the other spouse to improve their life in any and every way. That is the sin nature of the flesh. Remember, "That in one's flesh lies no good thing" (Romans 7:18).

I certainly hope that you are beginning to see the essence of this truth. Allow me for a moment to land on this issue with both feet to drive home this point.

When a man and a woman are married and if either one of them were never taught what true love really is, the love (from one if not both) that they will attempt to love each other with will most likely originate from their flesh. When this happens, the love generated cannot help but to become a selfish infatuated love; and it soon becomes undeniably apparent to the other party or to both parties. This selfish motivating corrupt love seeks

what it can gain from the other person and becomes a subtle form of prostitution; and It is displeasing to God (Romans 8:8). It may appear in the beginning stages of the relationship to be gratifying because of its novelty, but the unfortunate reality is that it will soon putrefy and become very distasteful and burdensome.
This is why divorce is so widespread.

This love (or lust) that is generated from your flesh says it is more blessed to receive than to give; while the love that is originated from your spirit says "It is more blessed to give than to receive"...Hmm? I've heard that somewhere before. Did someone else say that? Oh, yeah! Jesus was quoted saying that in Acts 20:35. The flesh is temporal because it will die one day and go back to the dust; so Anything that is produced from the flesh will also eventually perish (Romans 8:13). This is simply why "true love" can be derived only from your spirit.

If you are reading this book and are seeking a mate to marry and you are not walking in the spirit (Galatians 5:16), please for the sake of your own wellbeing learn how to operate out of your spirit and ask the Creator for a spouse that loves from their spirit source because true love cannot originate from the flesh. No one desires the love that originates from ones flesh. Not even those who offer love from the flesh desire it in return. It is despise by all. The truth is, when you sow to the flesh, you will reap corruption and eventual death. When you sow to the spirit you, will reap life, love and affection.

(Galatians 6:8) EVERYBODY SEEKS AFFECTION IN A RELATIONSHIP.

When a person is in the right relationship with the Creator, the spirit of that person becomes renewed. That individual has a responsibility to continue to walk in the spirit and be determined to walk in the newness of their transformed spirit mind (Romans 12:2). When this happens and when that person expresses love, it is given (and I emphasize that word given) out of their spirit, and it is a pure unselfish love, this love emulates God's love. The litmus test of true love is it always gives. John 3:16 states, "For God so loved the world that He gave his only begotten Son…"

Giving will always be synonymous with real love. 1 Corinthians 13:5 states, "…love seeks not its own." There is no selfish motive whatsoever from love that originates from the spirit. Let me clarify; Let us suppose you met a person that was patient and extremely kind. This person was never envious of others, and thought that conceit was the most immature thing in the world. This individual had perfect manners, they did things for you with absolutely no ulterior motive, and they seldom if ever were provoked to anger. This person never thought evil of you, they were never happy to see evil in any form, and constantly sought after truth. They helped you with all of your struggles, believed in you with all their heart, and sincerely hoped that every one of your endeavors were successful. They also fully committed themselves to helping you with you every trial that life has to throw at you. According to 1 Corinthians 13, I just described some of the characteristics of a person who expresses love originating from their spirit.

Sexual intercourse ("true" love making) in this type of marriage relationship is like consuming the sweet mingled wine that is pressed from the grapes of heavens vineyards...When consumed in abundance, one will find that it is righteously intoxicating and it only gets better with time.

If both parties are living and loving this way they will find themselves trying to out give each other in the marriage relationship. This is the kind of relationship that every person seeks, but only few achieve because of lack of proper knowledge and understanding. Sexual intercourse ("true" love making) in this type of marriage relationship is like consuming the hallowed sweet mingled wine that is pressed from the grapes of heavens vineyards. This heavenly vintage wine is abundantly stored in the sacred wine vats of paradise and beckons all to come and taste of her virtuous pleasure. When consumed in abundance, one will find it is righteously intoxicating and it only gets better with time. In this kind of marriage relationship, sex is a blessed holy act that is very pleasing to the Heavenly

Father. "This is wisdom that is freely given to all who will obey and adhere to the pathway of life.)

I stated this before and I cannot state it enough because it absolutely must be emphasized. Love that originates and is expressed from ones renewed spirit, is constantly seeking how to create a better life for others. This is indeed "true love". It was from this same spirit element that love, light and life itself originates. This love changes people's lives and hearts. Jesus said, "Greater love hath no man than this, that a man lay down his life for his friends" (John 15:13). One word jumps out at me from that statement, UNSELFISHNESS. There is no greater force in the universe than this type of love. One cannot fake this kind of love. The flesh can never produce this love. The Master, Jesus Christ, when He was on Earth operated in this love.

This love invokes the manifestation of heavenly angelic beings into the atmosphere. Unselfishness motivates this love. Those who operate in this love become human magnets, because they attract all of those who lack this life giving force. There is no greater power than this ultimate weapon. Demonic forces flee from this type of love because it casts out fear, the very thing they thrive on (1John 4:18). This is the love that Jesus referred to when He said, "...All the world will know that you are my disciples if you have loved one for another" (John 13:35). It was this love that sent Jesus Christ to cross to die for the sins of "**OTHERS.**" There is no law against this type of love. This love is forever lasting, it has no limit, it never stops growing, it will never cease, everyday it looks for more ways to express itself, and it is forever faithful. No living creature can resist this type of love.

Love originating from man's renewed spirit is God's love. This type of love creates a heavenly ambiance in a relationship. God is a spirit and those of us that love Him, love Him out of our spirit. Proverbs 20:27 says, "The spirit of a man is the candle of the Lord, searching the inward parts of the belly." This means that when God communicates with us he does it through our spirit; consequently true love can only originate from the God-like part of us... our spirit. God is eternal, "true love" is eternal, God is spirit and God is love. Man's soul is eternal, Man is a spirit and God has provided a way for mankind to experience this true eternal love. There is absolutely nothing in the world greater than "true love". This is the kind of love that will always overcome hate.

I cannot be repetitive enough in writing about this. I could go on for the next several chapters commenting on this everlasting topic of love, but for the sake of time and space, I will stop here. I just wish that more of us had a better understanding of this most wonderful eternal gift that we all crave.

CHAPTER SIX - *FAITH AND WISDOM*

> *Wisdom is as ancient and steadfast as the very throne of God itself. No amount of earthly logic or candor could ever equal it. It is always as new as it is old…. It is timeless and nothing be can added to it.*

Wisdom is as ancient and steadfast as the very throne of God itself. No amount of earthly logic or candor could ever equal it. It is always as new as it is old. It transcends cultures, ages, philosophies and ideologies. It is timeless and nothing can be added to it. Faith unlike wisdom constantly has to be added to in order for one to operate effectively in it. They work together in unison and are vital to one's spiritual development. It all starts with faith. Without faith, one can never receive wisdom because God is the giver of wisdom. (James 1:5-6) To ask of god one must have faith.

Hebrews 11:6 states, "But without faith *it is* impossible to please *him*: for he that cometh to God must believe that he is, and *that* he is a rewarder of them that diligently seek him" KJV. So remember it all begins with faith.

Just like there is life, health, healing, and strength in drinking pure water, so is their spiritual life health, healing and strength in drinking and consuming the words of divine wisdom and principle. Man is more spiritual then he is physical. This is because a man's spirit and soul lives forever. We as humans need to be more mindful of the things of the soul and spirit. These are eternal. I cannot assert this enough. I am deliberately reiterating this truth throughout this book to thoroughly emphasize this concern. The things that concern the soul and spirit are eternal; and the things that concern the flesh are temporary.

I have found that when one minds first the things of the spirit, and the soul, the things of the body (flesh) will rightly align themselves with the things of the soul and spirit. Most people; however, endeavor to mind and engage themselves in the things of the flesh, thus becoming a slave to the things of the flesh. Paul the Apostle put it this way, "Walk in the spirit, so that you will not fulfill the lust of the flesh." Galatians 5:16

The flesh is a horrible master, but it is a wonderful servant. When a man's flesh is in control of his spirit, he becomes enslaved, bound, and shackled. He thinks that he is in control of his own ship on the ocean of life; but in reality the ravenous waves on the broad sea are tossing and tattering him and he is unconsciously headed for disaster and more than likely an ultimately death. This is the unfortunate fate of many who walk this earthly plain.

Now let's look at the flipside of this scenario. When a man walks in the spirit, he begins to live and experience true freedom. He has mastery over his body and his emotions. He is no longer a slave to his flesh but he becomes the servant to his spirit. His flesh gets put in check when his spirit is in control. By not walking in the flesh, a man puts himself in a position to build up his spirit.

Just how does a person build up his or her spirit? I'm glad you asked. Well, just as you build physical muscle through the process of resistance, so does one build up the spirit by the same method. It is done by resistance. At all costs, one must resist the works of the flesh. Just what are the works of the flesh? The best illustration that I can give is what Paul the Apostle, states in Galatians 5:19 – 23, "*19* Now the works of the flesh are manifeste, which are *these;* a
Adultery, fornication uncleanness, lasciviousness,
20 Idolatry, witchcraft, hatred, variance, emulations, wrath, strife, sedition, heresies,
21 Envying, murders, drunkenness, revellings and suchlike: of which I tell you before, as I have also told *you* in time past, that they which do such things, shall not inherit the kingdom of God.
22 But the fruit of the spirit is love, joy, peace, longsuffering, goodness, faith,
23 Meekness, temperance: against such there is no law" KJV.

Whenever the word law is mentioned, there is always a threat of bondage if one violates the law. If this is true, then the opposite of this absolutely has to be true. There is total freedom and liberty if one abides by the law. Notice above in Galatians 5:23 where it states that there is no law against the fruit of the spirit. This proves "that there is total freedom in righteousness." (Galatians 5:1)

Now in order to produce this righteous fruit, seedlings of righteous must be planted. This is accomplished through the process of walking in the spirit.

In the early stages of walking in the spirit, after the planting process, the nurturing stage must follow in order for the seedlings to mature into fruit bearing trees.

This all happens by an act of your will. This is what I call "willed action." Through the act of a man's willful obedience and submission to the Creator by faith, God, our Creator has made it possible for a man to sit in heavenly places and experience eternal results while living in his body here on Earth. (Eph: 2:6)

It is my earnest prayer that through this applied knowledge, you are beginning to understand the relationship between faith and wisdom.

PROVERBS CH. 8

Listen to what Proverbs 8 says, "*1* Does not wisdom cry out, and understanding put forth her voice?
2 She takes her stand on the top of the high hill, beside the way, where the paths meet.
3 She cries out at the gates, at the entry of the city, at the coming in at the doors,
4 'To you, O men, I call; and my voice *is* to the sons of man.
5 O you simple ones, understand wisdom: and, you fools, be of an understanding heart.
6 Listen; for I will speak of excellent things; and from the opening of my lips *will come* right things. *7* For my mouth will speak truth; and wickedness *is* an abomination to my lips.
8 All the words of my mouth *are* in righteousness; *there is* nothing crooked or perverse in them.
9 They *are* all plain to him that understands, and right to them that find knowledge.
10 Receive my instruction, and not silver; and knowledge rather than choice gold'.
11 For wisdom *is* better than rubies, and all the things one may desire cannot be compared with her.

12 'I wisdom dwell with prudence, and find out knowledge of witty intentions.
13 The fear of the Lord *is* to hate evil, pride and arrogance, and the evil way, and the perverse mouth, I hate.

14 Counsel *is* mine, and sound wisdom, I *am* understanding; I have strength.

15 By me kings reign, and rulers decree justice.

16 By me princes rule, and nobles, *even* all the judges of the earth.

17 I love those who love me, and those who seek me diligently will find me.

18 Riches and honor *are* with me; enduring riches and righteousness.

19 My fruit *is* better than gold, yes, than fine gold, and my revenue than choice silver.

20 I traverse the way of righteousness, in the midst of the paths of justice,

21 That I may cause those who love me to inherit wealth, that I may fill their treasuries.

22 The Lord possessed me at the beginning of His way, before His works of old.

23 I have been established from everlasting, from the beginning, before there was ever an earth.

24 When *there were* no depths I was brought forth; when *there were* no fountains abounding with water

25 Before the mountains were settled, before the hills I was brought forth,

26 While as yet He had not made the earth, nor the fields, nor the primeval dust of the world.

27 When He prepared the heavens, I *was* there, when He drew a circle on the face of the deep,

28 When He established the clouds above, when He strengthened the fountains of the deep,

29 When He assigned to the sea its limit, so that the waters would not transgress His command, when He marked out the foundations of the earth,

30 Then I was beside Him *as* a master craftsman; and I was daily *His* delight, rejoicing always before Him;

31 Rejoicing in His inhabited world; and my delight *was* with the sons of men.

32 Now therefore listen to me, my children: for blessed *are those who* keep my ways.

33 Hear instruction, and be wise, and do not disdain it.

34 Blessed *is* the man who listens to me, watching daily at my gates, waiting at the posts of my doors.

35 For whomever finds me finds life, and obtains favor from the Lord *36* But he who sins against me wrongs his own soul, all those who hate me love death.'" NKJV.

I am reminded of a phrase that my mother taught me. "Love what wisdom loves, hate what wisdom hates, and you will enjoy what wisdom enjoys."

After reading this, I am reminded of a phrase that my mother taught me, "Love what wisdom loves, hate what wisdom hates, and you will enjoy what wisdom enjoys."

Far too many people run life's gauntlet without the protection of faith and wisdom. Wisdom and faith are both spiritual laws. They are universal laws. Everything starts with faith; and the law of wisdom promises life to those who choose to surrender their earthly astuteness to its eternal ways and principles. Listen to what King Solomon states in Proverbs 3:13-18,

13 "Blessed *is* the man *who* finds wisdom, the man who gains understanding.
14 For she *is* more profitable than silver and yields better returns than gold.
15 She *is* more precious than rubies, nothing you desire can compare with her.
16 Long life *is* in her right hand; in her left hand are riches and honor.
17 Her ways *are* pleasant ways, and all her paths *are* peace.
18 She *is* a tree of life to those who embrace her, those who lay hold of her will be blessed." NKJV.

Those who consume, embrace, and govern their lives by these timeless precepts are destined for success. (Proverbs 3:1-10).

Most people live under the misconception that success is something that comes from outside of yourself. Let me reassure you, this simply is untrue. Do not let anyone mislead you. Success comes from within you. Success starts with a decision; just as failure is accomplished by lack of a decision. A large part of true success is finding your assignment and pursuing it with all that is within you. When you commit yourself to your calling; you will find that the hard work that accompanies YOUR WORK becomes extremely enjoyable; partly because this is WHAT YOU WERE CREATED TO DO. This is when you begin to live your life from the inside out, the way you were ordained by our Creator.

If your calling is to be a lawyer, you have no business trying to be a carpenter because your father was a carpenter or because a mentor pushed you in that direction. You may even experience a degree of success in a profession that you were not designed to practice; but you will not feel that sense of gratification that only your true calling can give you. I will guarantee you this, if you are working in a profession that you are not created for, you will work harder than your colleagues, and you will feel like that occupation goes against the very grain of your soul. What also happens when you do not exercise the innate God given gifts and talents within yourself, you become a stumbling block to yourself and others. This is the epitome of selfishness and disobedience. Remember, Paul the apostle said; "If we sow to our own selfish desires, we will reap **only** corruption." (Galatians 6:8) Not only is this counterproductive to you and all associated with you, most tragically, it is displeasing to our Creator. God is pleased when a man or a woman finds their calling and become the best that they can be at it. When we operate in our God given calling, and when we operate in the innate gifts and talents betrothed upon us at birth, we become a blessing and an inspiration to all around us;

and the best part of this is that this is very pleasing to our Creator. So, if you are reading this and you feel this is speaking to you, make SURE to ask the Heavenly Father to show you who you are, and continue to pray earnestly in faith to receive the revelation concerning your life.

CHAPTER SEVEN - *FAITH IS A VERB*

According to world book dictionary a verb is, "A word that tells what is or what is done" (notice that it is in the present tense). Back in grade school we were all taught that a verb is a word that describes action. This is just as faith is. Faith becomes activated when it is ignited through some form of action. In the story of the Bible, in the account of the children of Israel crossing over the Red Sea, there was a great illustration of this. The Israelites were being led by Moses out of the land of Egypt, their came a point during this exodus when they found themselves with the Red Sea in front of them and the vast Egyptian army behind them. They were plainly stated, caught between "…a sword and a wet place".

It was up to Moses, their fearless leader, to get them out of this quandary of sorts. It was only when Moses (a man of faith) in faith lifted up his staff (a form of action) that something happened. Most of us know what happened. The Red Sea divided and the Israelites walked over on dry land (Exodus 14:16). I will venture to say that if Moses did nothing, nothing would have happened. Indecently, this account is stated in Hebrews 11:29. This chapter in Hebrews is what I call the "Great Hall of Faith" chapter in the Holy Bible.

It is a proven fact that an individual's faith, is in direct correlation with their actions. Let me give you a for instance. If I told you that it was raining one hundred dollar bills outside right now and you believed me; it would become immediately apparent, because there would be an instant response in your actions. I say that to make this point. Many people often pray, and during their prayer they will be thinking to themselves, *I really don't think God is going to answer this prayer because this situation seems too impossible.* If this describes your praying habits, please stop this immediately. This type of praying is not only a waste of time, and counterproductive, but it displeases the Creator. The answers to prayers only come when your thoughts, while you are praying, coincide with your actions and your confessions when you get up from praying. This bears worth repeating. The answers to your prayers only come when your thoughts, while you are praying, coincide with your actions and your confessions when you get up from praying.

So, if and when the next time you are praying, you find yourself not in line with this prayer principle, immediately get up, and do the following. Realign and regroup your thoughts, begin to pray and see the very thing that you are praying for in your mind already happening, pray to its end, and then seal it with gratitude by continuously thanking the Creator in earnest for it already being accomplished. When you get up from praying, say to yourself that whatever it is that you just prayed for is on its way. Then most importantly, go out and look for that thing that you just prayed for in a spirit of expectation and gratitude. The more gratitude that you express toward the Creator, for already answering your prayer, the stronger your faith becomes and the faster that thing that you are praying for will manifest. Remember, true gratitude always propels and seals faith. It is our only God given attribute that accelerates the process of our prayers being answered. Gratitude and faith together work hand in hand.

Let me clarify what I am saying this way. In the natural when you go to the department store and you see an item that you want, you can put a down payment on that item. The item is only given to you when you finish paying the balance. The faster you pay the balance the faster you receive your merchandise. It is very similar in the spirit realm. Your initial prayer in this case represents your down payment for your prayer request. Now by faith it is already yours, but you have not yet received it. Gratitude represents the balance for that initial prayer request. The more gratitude that is attached to that prayer request, the faster you will receive the answer. What genuine gratitude does in the spirit realm is that it works conjointly with your faith and hastens the return on the things that you pray for.

> *In the spirit world, there is no such thing as time and space as we know it in our world. Ten minutes in that world could be the equivalent of ten years in our world. Gratitude is the great equalizer between both worlds.*

This is where most people miss it. This answers the reason why many people pray and never receive answers to their prayers. They make their "prayer down payment request" and never send in the balance. You must understand that <u>in the spirit world, there is no such thing as time and space as we know it in our world. Ten minutes in that world could be the equivalent of ten years in our world. Gratitude is the great equalizer between both worlds.</u> You simply must have a genuine attitude of gratitude. The more gratitude you express, the higher the octane grade will be in the petroleum that your prayer travels on. You control the speedometer to the answer to your prayers with your measure of gratitude. This is a hidden truth unknown to many.

Faith and gratitude when combined create a harmonious spiritual musical chord that allows your prayer to travel on from Earth to Heaven. That prayer chord is in synchronization with all of creation and resonates throughout the universe and into the presence of God the Father Creator. That faith polished prayer travels on the wings of faith, and He (the Creator) is moved by this type of faith. No man can please God without faith (Hebrews11:6). He cannot help but command the ministering spirits (angels) Hebrews 11:14, to grant the requests of all that operate by faith who are in harmony with his will. The reason for this is, because both faith and gratitude are predestined by God.

When you use this prayer principle, you will see it works every time. Remember that faith without works is dead. This only again proves the law of sowing and reaping and that your outer world of circumstance is controlled by your inner world of thought.

To put it all in perspective, I have formulated from the Holy Scriptures on how to get what you pray for from the heavenly spirit realm to the earthly realm. This is where most people fail because they do not know how to execute the procedure of prayer. Here is the process in a step by step formula.

1. Pray and make your request known to the Heavenly Father. (Philippians 4:6)
2. While you are praying, see the thing happening and already done. (Mark 11:22 -24)
3. After you see it happen in your mind, thank the Heavenly Father for already creating it for you in the spirit realm and thank him for answering your prayer and for giving it to you. Always start out the prayer with thanksgiving to the Father Creator. (Matthew 11:25)
4. Then get up from praying, write a positive confession of what you just prayed for .Make sure that it is written in the present tense. Make sure that you state in your confession that it has been granted, and that it is on its way. (Romans 4:17) Do not be misled by what you see. Remember faith comes by hearing (Romans 10:17) and doubt comes by seeing. We walk by faith not by sight. (2nd Cor. 5:7)
5. Then immediately go after what you just prayed for. (Mark 11:23). All the while when you are inwardly

repeating your confession to yourself and confessing it into your spirit (saying it to yourself several hundreds of times a day if you have to). A very effective way to do this is to put your confession on a portable mp3 player or make a CD recording, carry it around with you and listen to it as often as possible. If it was a new car that you prayed for, in your mind, see yourself driving that car, putting gas in it, parking it etc....

6. After it is fused into your spirit repeat it out loud as often as possible. Above all, make sure that you stay in an attitude of gratitude toward your creator for already answering your prayers. If you stay in this attitude of gratitude, you will see the speedy manifestation of what you are praying for. As Jesus said, the Father already knows you have need of these things. (Luke 12:30). This is just a test of your faith for you to pass and to grow spiritually. I have practiced this principle on many occasions and it works.

Upon execution of this principle you will loose in the earth and heavenly territories your results. (Matt 16:19) They are on their way. Just remember to maintain a genuine attitude of gratitude.

Jesus States in Matthew 16:19, "And I will give you the keys of the Kingdom of heaven; and whatever you bind on earth will be bound in heaven; and whatever you loose on earth will be loosed in heaven." NKJV

The really wonderful thing about faith is that it is unlimited. It permits those of us that understand its application to dream big dreams and to overcome and succeed in whatever befalls us. What do I mean when I say that? Let's say for instance, you are reading this book and you are extremely wealthy. The problem that you may have might be a terminal illness. You may have been to several physicians and they all confirmed you have at best, three months to live. You find yourself in a situation where your wealth is useless to you. This is where the unlimited benefits of faith kick in. You can apply the faith principle and make a total recovery from your illness. You may be famous, powerful, and well respected in the eyes of the world and as wonderful as all of these features are, they are limited. Here is where faith is needed. Faith is LIMITLESS and one can and will achieve what they need to achieve in this life through the application of faith.

I do not wish to mislead any of my readers by sending any type of subliminal message here that once you begin to operate in the laws of faith that life becomes easy; no, not at all. It will seem more difficult in the beginning stages because the enemy of your soul operates under spiritual law and understands that these spiritual principles when applied HAVE to work for you. He will try to discourage you on every side even before you begin to make progress. I apologize if I have misled you in that regard. What I am strongly suggesting and saying is that once a person takes the initiative and makes up in their mind they are going to make a conscious effort to <u>add daily to their given measure of faith</u>, from that moment on; life becomes a "heaven" of a lot more predictable. What am I saying? The best way that I can illustrate this point is by the following analogy.

Your applied faith upon those desolate circumstances will be your evidence that the sun will reappear on your pathway and that your victory is just a clouds passing.

Most of us have seen the skies just before a terrible rain storm. The type of rain storm that I am referring to does not happen very often. This type of storm is when during midday, the clouds are enormously thick, and it makes the mid-afternoon appear to resemble the late evening. It may be 2:00 P.M. in the afternoon, but at the time it could pass for 9:00 P.M. at night. I am sure most readers can identify with this situation. Even though it may look like it is 9:00 P.M. at night when it is only 2:00 P.M in the afternoon, the TRUTH is that it is still daylight, AND THE SUN IS STILL SHINING IN its FULLNESS BEHIND THE CLOUDS.

It matters not what the conditions look like at the moment. THE EVIDENCE that I have, is that according to the watch on my wrist, it is 2:00 p.m. in the afternoon. The NATURAL LAWS that govern nature, give me the full assurance that behind the shadow of the clouds the sun by NATURAL LAW will shine for another four to five hours regardless of how it may look at the moment. I know very shortly, the skies will clear and that the sun (that was always there) will reappear.

Now to catch the full revelation of this picture, we have to look at Hebrews 11:1 again. "Now faith is the substance of things hoped for, the evidence of things not seen." Just as in the scenario of the rain storm, in the same way do we apply the faith principle when the storms and dark clouds of life come to cast their shadows over the circumstances of our lives. Remember that we walk by faith and not by sight,(2nd Corinthians.5:7) Even though it may appear that all may be lost and that hope has vanished beyond the horizon during this isolated time period of your life. We can take full assurance in the TRUTH that SPIRITUAL LAWS govern all of life and it really does not matter what the conditions may look like. What matters is we understand that the "SON" who shines in HIS brightness (Rev 22:16) despite the dark clouds always cares deeply about you and your situation and that your applied faith upon those desolate circumstances will be your EVIDENCE that the sun will reappear on your pathway and that your victory is just a clouds passing.

Again look closely at the first two words of the verse of Hebrews 11:1, "Now faith…" Let us stop there for just a moment; "Now faith", meaning right now. The implication here is that it is an immediate reaction. Remember, that in the spirit realm there is no time or space. So, this means that when a person in the Earth realm prays in faith, there is an instant reaction in the spirit realm as to that person's request being received. Listen to the verse very closely "NOW FAITH is the SUBSTANCE of things hoped for, the EVIDENCE of things not seen." Look at the three key words italicized here, *"NOW FAITH SUBSTANCE* and *EVIDENCE."* The insinuation here is, NOW FAITH equals SUBSTANCE AND EVIDENCE. To better illustrate this, listen to what the Apostle Paul says in Romans 4:17, "(As it is written, I have made you a Father of many nations, in the presence of him who he believed—God who gives life to the dead which calls those things which do not exist as though they were)" NKJV. When we operate in faith, God gives us the privilege of doing just what Paul is saying here. Calling those things which do not exist as though they do exist; because at that moment in the spirit realm, your faith filled words created what you called into existence. When a man or a woman of faith prays or commands something according to God's will, it is actually created at that very moment in the spirit realm. Now in the Earth realm, it appears that nothing has taken place, but in the spirit realm because time does not exist, it took place at the moment of the persons faith driven prayer request. The individual's faith is the substance and evidence of the reality of their spoken word.

I certainly hope that you are beginning to see how this all ties in. I realize that for several readers, this may be something you have never heard before and I do not wish anyone to think this is some type of magic or the like. This is nothing of the sort. What this is, is law.

I speak with unshakable confidence concerning spiritual law. It has been tested and tried and it has stood the test of not only time but eternity as well. Most individuals are familiar with only the natural laws that govern the Earth which are restricted only to the natural world. Remember that these are eternal laws; they pervade both the spirit world and the natural world. Few people (by ratio the vast numbers that live on Earth) understand and operate in these laws. God the Creator purposed for all of mankind to live by these laws. These principles are perfect. They lead to the pathway of life, Matthew 7:13. They are in harmony with all of God's creation. It is my hope and my prayer that every reader will familiarize themselves with them and will live by the life giving precepts they contain.

CHAPTER EIGHT - *FAITH AND THOUGHT*

Just what effect does faith have on our thoughts?

To effectively answer this question, let's go back to what I stated at the beginning of chapter three.

"Every thought that we think carries energy with it. The energy that each thought carries is either that of strength, (faith) or weakness (fear)"

If I can, allow me to illustrate it like this. Every one of us has two bank accounts in our minds. One account is called faith, and the other account is called fear. Every day, we make deposits into one or the other of these accounts. There is always room in each account so that they can never be full. Over the process of time, which ever account that we deposit the majority of our thoughts into, will be the account that we will withdraw from in the time of crisis. This again proves the law of sowing and reaping. I cannot this point enough. KEEP YOU MIND PREGNANT WITH THOUGHTS OF FAITH.

Everybody has faith. The reason for this is because everybody was <u>given a measure of faith,</u> (Romans 12:3) whether we want to accept it or not. Either you are going to consciously use your will to direct your thoughts in a positive way and have your inner world control your outer world; or like most, you are going to let your mind wander on the sea of life and let the outer control you and your inner world. It is your choice. I cannot drive home this point enough. Again, if you do not consciously take control of your thoughts and your inner world, the choice of the outer world controlling your life and circumstances will be made for you. I will guarantee you will not enjoy the results. Everything starts with a decision.

> *If there is the good fight of faith, there has to be the "bad fight of doubt". Remember that everything has an opposite.*

The Creator gave us the option to choose what outcome we will have manifested in our life by consciously choosing the thoughts that we constantly dwell on. Any inner thoughts planted in the substance soil of faith whether they be negative or positive will produce the exact outward conditions in that person's life. This is again the ageless law of sowing and reaping. Paul the Apostle in 1 Timothy 6:12 wrote, "Fight the good fight of faith, lay hold on eternal life, whereunto thou are called." The good fight of faith is the positive fight of faith; the good fight of faith lays hold on eternal life resulting in a positive predictable outcome.

If there is the good fight of faith, there has to be "the bad fight of doubt". Remember that everything has an opposite. The bad fight of doubt is obviously the dreadful or the opposite side of faith which ultimately lays hold on eternal damnation. Doubt is the concierge for failure and destruction. One is always fighting a losing battle when consumed with doubt. Doubt should always be guarded against and never be allowed to take up lodging in one's mind. Faith and victory are always synonymous; and desired results are always forthcoming when faith is allowed to be the standard of ones thinking. That is why it is called the "GOOD FIGHT OF FAITH". It is always going to be a struggle that is why it is called a fight. Often times it is a knock down drag out fight, but it is still called the **good fight** because when fighting with faith one cannot fail!

Think of faith like this. Faith is like a bonfire. In order to get it started, you have to ignite it with a spark, which represents action. (faith without works or "without action" is dead). Then you have to continually feed it the proper substance (remember that faith is a substance) to keep it burning. The more you feed it with the right substance, the brighter, stronger, and more powerful it becomes. You then have to as often as possible continue to prune it by removing the dead ashes that have already burned (this would be indicative to past victories) which the fire can no longer live on; because they have run their course. Brand new dry twigs (which would be indicative to daily new faith assignments) or new fuel must be added frequently in order for the process of burning to continue and for the individual to continue to receive the benefits of the fire. If these acts are not regulated, the fire will go into a smoldering state or a sleeping state (remember faith must be kept awake) providing little to no benefit to the individual. The point here is to always "keep the fire burning."

Please allow me to close this short chapter with an idealistic thought. What if the masses of adults living in the world today were keeping their minds pregnant with thoughts of faith? What type of a world do you think we would have? Do you think that countries would have time to be at war with each other? Do you think that people would be envious of one another? If this were the case, racism and poverty would be eradicated from the earth. I believe this because of what Jesus stated in the Lord's Prayer when He prayed, "Thy Kingdom come, Thy will be done on earth as *it is* in heaven". If this were indeed the case, I strongly believe, there would be little distinction between Heaven and Earth.

CHAPTER NINE - *THE HALL OF FAITH*

I cannot complete this book without honoring the members of the Great Hall of Faith. This is found in Hebrews 11, of the Holy Bible. I understand that some readers have no idea of what I am saying, so for their sake, I will quote the whole chapter. Before I do, I must dispel the notion that these individuals were super heroes. They were everyday ordinary people just like you and me. The difference was that they understood that they were given a <u>measure of faith; and they made the decision (just as we can today) to add to their God given measure of faith</u>; as a result we are reading about them still today. I love this chapter because it serves as a constant reminder that we all have the ability to do great exploits and that greatness is not reserved for an elite few. Every time when you are faced with a seemingly impossible task, the challenge is extended, and it is opportunity in disguise to add to your <u>given measure of faith</u>, just as these did.

1 "Now faith is the substance of things hoped for, the evidence of things not seen.
2 For by it the elders obtained a good testimony.
3 Through faith we understand that the worlds were framed by the word of God, so that the things which are seen were not made of things which are visible.
4 By faith Abel offered to God a more excellent sacrifice than Cain, through which he obtained witness that he was righteous, God testifying of his gifts; and through it he being dead still speaks.

5 By faith Enoch was taken away so that he did not see death, and was not found, because God had taken him; for before he was taken he had this testimony, that he pleased God.

6 But without faith *it is* impossible to please *Him*; for he who comes to God must believe that He is, and *that* He is a rewarder of those who diligently seek Him.

7 By faith Noah, being warned of God of things not yet seen, moved with fear, prepared an ark for the saving of his household; by which he condemned the world, and became heir of the righteousness which is according to faith.

8 By faith Abraham, obeyed when he was called to go out to the place which he would receive as an inheritance and he went out, not knowing where he was going.

9 By faith he dwelt in the land of promise, as *in* a foreign country, dwelling in tents with Isaac and Jacob, the heirs with him of the same promise;

10 For he waited for the city which has foundations, whose builder and maker *is* God.

11 By faith Sarah herself also received strength to conceive seed, and she bore a child when she was past the age, because she judged Him faithful who had promised.

12 Therefore from one man, and him as good as dead, were born *as many* as the stars of the sky in multitude-- innumerable as the sand which is by the seashore.

13 These all died in faith, not having received the promises, but having seen them afar off were assured of *them*, embraced *them* and confessed that they were strangers and pilgrims on the earth.

14 For those who say such things declare plainly that they seek a homeland.

15 And truly, if they had called to mind that *country* from which they had come out, they would have had opportunity to return.

16 But now they desire a better, that is, a heavenly country; therefore, God is not ashamed to be called their God, for He has prepared a city for them.

17 By faith Abraham, when he was tested, offered up Isaac, and he who had received the promises offered up his only begotten *son*,

18 Of whom it was said, 'In Isaac your seed shall be called,'

19 Concluding that God *was* able to raise *him* up, even from the dead; from which he also received him in a figurative sense.

20 By faith Isaac blessed Jacob and Esau concerning things to come.

21 By faith Jacob, when he was dying, blessed each of the sons of Joseph, and worshiped, *leaning* on the top of his staff.

22 By faith Joseph, when he was dying, made mention of the departure of the children of Israel, and gave instructions concerning his bones.

23 By faith Moses, when he was born, was hidden three months by his parents, because they saw *he was* a beautiful child; and they were not afraid of the king's command.

24 By faith Moses, when he became of age, refused to be called the son of Pharaoh's daughter;

25 Choosing rather to suffer affliction with the people of God, than to enjoy the passing pleasures of sin,

26 Esteeming the reproach of Christ greater riches than the treasures in Egypt; for he looked to the reward.

27 By faith he forsook Egypt, not fearing the wrath of the king; for he endured as seeing Him who is invisible.

28 By faith he kept the Passover and the sprinkling of blood, lest he who destroyed the firstborn should touch them.

29 By faith they passed through the Red Sea as by dry *land*, whereas the Egyptians, attempting to do so, were drowned.

30 By faith the walls of Jericho fell down, after they were encircled for seven days.

31 By faith the harlot Rahab did not perish with those who did not believe, when she had received the spies with peace.

32 And what more shall I say? For the time would fail me to tell of Gideon and Barak and Samson and Jephthah, also of David and Samuel and the prophets:

33 Who through faith subdued kingdoms, worked righteousness, obtained promises, stopped the mouths of lions,

34 Quenched the violence of fire, escaped the edge of the sword, out of weakness were made strong, became valiant in battle, turned to flight the armies of the aliens.

35 Women received their dead raised to life again; and others were tortured, not accepting deliverance, that they might obtain a better resurrection;

36 Still others had trial of mockings and scourgings, yes, and of chains and imprisonment;

37 They were stoned, they were sawn in two, were tempted, and were slain with the sword; they wandered about in sheepskins and goatskins, being destitute, afflicted, tormented,

38 (Of whom the world was not worthy;) they wandered *in* deserts and mountains, *in* dens and caves of the earth.

39 And all these, having obtained a good testimony through faith, did not receive the promise,

40 God having provided something better for us, that they should not be made perfect apart from us." NKJV

You see when you live like this, you live with expectation. It is just like a woman who is pregnant. She is living; **expecting** to soon deliver a child. Why can she expect is this? Because the Laws of nature dictate that if she is indeed pregnant, that in the process of time, she will produce a baby. So in order to accomplish all that you are to accomplish in this life, your thoughts have to be pregnant with faith. When this happens, you cannot help but live expecting things to happen. Why is this? Because **spiritual law** dictates that if indeed you are living with pregnant thoughts of faith, that in the process of time, you too will produce what you are expecting. Remember, Spiritual law gave birth to all natural and scientific laws which means that spiritual law is far more superior to natural and scientific laws.

A foot note to this chapter. If you were to go back and do some research on these individuals, you will notice that there is a common denominator to every one of these stories. That one common thread that is interwoven through the fabric of all of these accounts is this. At the time when all of these honorees where called on to do great exploits, none of them had all of the resources at hand to accomplish the seemingly impossible. In order for these people to accomplish what they did, prior to these events they had to live with pregnant thoughts of faith, and in the process of time, the day of expectation (or delivery) for them came in the form of each account that you just read in Hebrews 11.They all used the ultimate resource of faith to create the material resources needed to accomplish what they needed to do; just as we can today.

CHAPTER TEN - *MURPHYS (f LAW)*

I entitled this chapter MURPHYS (f LAW) for a distinctive reason. Before we thrash out the details concerning "Murphy's Law" I did a little research as to who this man was, and how this phrase gained so much notoriety. For those of you who are unfamiliar with "Murphy's Law" it states, anything that can go wrong will go wrong. In my opinion this guy has probably caused more hindrance to the development of individual's dreams than anyone else in history. Why do I say that? He has contaminated the minds or the thinking centers of countless millions, if not billions of people worldwide. The irony of this is that what he said is true. In my opinion, what he singlehandedly did was to sabotage the positive thinking process. Murphy's Law is faith in reverse. This is the law of attraction in reverse that works against an individual for the detriment and not for the betterment of the person. Remember, that there is an opposite negative side to every law that exists. This is why I call it Murphy's
(f LAW) or better said, Murphy's mistake.

- The following article was excerpted from *The Desert Wings*, March 3, 1978

- Murphy's Law ("If anything can go wrong, it will") was born at Edwards Air Force Base in 1949 at North Base.

- It was named after Captain Edward A. Murphy; an engineer working on Air Force Project MX981, (a project) designed to see how much sudden deceleration a person can stand in a crash.

- One day, after finding that a transducer was wired wrong, he cursed the technician responsible and said, "If there is any way to do it wrong, he'll find it."

- The contractor's project manager kept a list of "laws" and added this one, which he called Murphy's Law.

- Actually, what he did was take an old law that had been around for years in a more basic form and gave it a name.

- Shortly afterwards, the Air Force doctor (Dr. John Paul Stapp), who rode a sled on the deceleration track to a stop, pulling 40 Gs, gave a press conference. He said their good safety record on the project was due to a firm belief in Murphy's Law and in the necessity to try and circumvent it.

- Aerospace manufacturers picked it up and used it widely in their ads during the next few months, and soon it was being quoted in many news and magazine articles. Murphy's Law was born.

Let's examine this statement. "WHAT EVER CAN GO WRONG, WILL GO WRONG" This statement is beyond true if you choose to operate on that side of the law. This statement when accepted and mentally embraced invokes the law of attraction. I call it Murphy's (f LAW) because instead of directing people to the positive side of the law of attraction, he directs people to the negative side of the law of attraction. What a tragedy. In my opinion if anybody ever needed a paradigm shift, it was this guy Murphy.

What if instead of saying, "WHAT EVER CAN GO WRONG, WILL GO WRONG" he said, "WHAT EVER WILL GO RIGHT WILL GO RIGHT". IT IS THE EXACT SAME LAW IN EFFECT, ONLY IN REVERSE. Both statements work. It is up to us to decide which one we want working for us. This is mind contamination. I shudder to think of how much faith this statement has destroyed in the minds and hearts of people worldwide. My hope is that manuscripts as the one you are now reading will get into the hands and hearts of people worldwide to help negate many negative sayings like this one, that only hinder people's faith and progress.

The great catastrophe here is that individuals often make these sayings without intentionally trying to cause harm, but much harm is done out of ignorance. This reminds me of the support group, Alcoholics Anonymous. For those of you reading this book outside of the United States, here in America we have a support group called Alcoholics Anonymous. From what I understand, whenever a meeting is held, the members are instructed to give their name and state that they are an alcoholic. In my opinion, I feel that this is wrong. I If I had my way, I would change that. Why? I'm glad you asked. The reason is simple. Positive confession is a vital part of the faith process. Overcoming any addiction is a done deal when one applies faith.

I believe that I understand what A.A. is trying to do. They are getting people out of denial by having them admit that they have a drinking problem. This is good, necessary, and it has its place. Once a person confesses and understands that they have a problem, they should be taken from that point, to the point of overcoming and ultimately to the point of victory. I cannot help right now of thinking about Moses. Early on in his life he was a murderer. If he kept confessing to himself that he was a murderer, he would have stayed in that mindset and who knows how many people he would have killed during the course of his life. If this were the case, we would not have had the first five books of the Holy Bible. That's really something to think about.

CHAPTER ELEVEN - *FAITH AND THE PLACEBO EFFECT*

In the field of medical science, doctors often issue what they call a placebo to usually terminally ill patients. Before I comment on this topic let us look at the standard definition for this word. Placebo: (noun) **something prescribed for a patient that contains no medicine, but is given for the positive psychological effect it may have because the patient believes he or she is receiving treatment.**

The following article appeared in the "FRONTAL CORTEX ONLINE MAGAZINE" JUNE 16, 2008 WRITTEN BY JONAH LEHRER.

"There's so much unexplained stuff. I don't quite understand the scientific explanation of the placebo effect. What is the core of that? The fact that the placebo effect exists is a fact, but what is it? We have no idea. I love that. I even love that with regard to the home-court advantage in sports. What is that? It's connected to a belief system. Both things, the placebo and the home-court effect, are a belief system that we can turn thought into actual biological function. In and of itself, that's something that science says is not possible. But you can document it.

On the one hand, I agree that science has real epistemological limits. And yet, the placebo effect - or any other example that involves a "belief system" or "thought" becoming "actual biological function" - is a terrible example of such limitations. There is nothing inherently mysterious about a psychological thought impacting the activity of neurons. That's what thoughts do. (What else would they do? It's like being amazed that my strokes on keyboard impact the activity of silicon Microchips somewhere inside a computer.) As for the placebo effect...The precise mechanisms of the effect have been well documented.

Tor Wager, a neuroscientist at Columbia University, has probably done the definitive brain imaging study. His experiment was brutally straightforward: he gave college students electrical shocks while they were stuck in an MRI machine. Half of the people were then supplied with a fake pain-relieving cream. Even though the cream had no analgesic properties - it was just a hand moisturizer - people given the pretend cream said the shocks were significantly less painful. The placebo effect eased their suffering. Wager then imaged the specific parts of the brain that controlled this psychological process. He discovered that the placebo effect depended on the prefrontal cortex, the center of "rational," conscious thought. When people were told that they'd just received a pain-relieving cream, their frontal lobes responded by inhibiting the activity of the emotional brain areas (like the insula) that normally respond to pain. Because people expected to experience less pain, they ended up experiencing less pain.

"I agree with Shyamalan that there is something inherently wondrous about the idea of conscious thoughts and ethereal daydreams being able to directly influence squirts of neurotransmitter and the electrical firings of neurons. But that's only because we are natural dualists, innately programmed to believe in a metaphysical soul".

I researched this article for the sole purpose of proving that the placebo effect is the perfect illustration of the law of faith being executed. Note in the article where Doctor Wagner points out. (Before you read his quote keep in mind what Romans 10: 17 says, "That faith comes by hearing") "When people were told that they'd just received a pain –relieving cream, their frontal lobes responded by inhibiting the activity of the emotional brain areas (like the insula) that normally respond to pain. Because people expected to experience less pain, they ended up experiencing less pain". This speaks for itself.

After reading that report, let us take another look At Hebrews 11: 1 "Now faith is the substance of things hoped for, the evidence of things not seen." I think that this is the perfect snap shot of the principle of faith in action. Spiritual law was never meant to be complicated or confusing.

It is my belief if medical science would humble itself and would except spiritual law for what it is (pure truth and factual evidence), that technology as we know it would become light years ahead of where we are today. It is my prayer and hopes that before my tenure on the Earth is concluded, medical science and natural science will embrace the truth of spiritual law for the enlightenment and future advancement of mankind.

CHAPTER TWELVE - *FINAL THOUGHTS ON FAITH*

One of the greatest questions of antiquity is whether or not the fountain of youth does in fact exist. Explorers throughout the ages have traveled the world over in search for this ever so elusive cascade of perennial life. Modern day cosmetic ointments claim to have age retarding potions to help sustain ones youthful appearance. Some will tell you if you bathe in the mineral springs of a particular exotic location that your youth will be somehow invigorated from within. I am sure that you have heard your share of continuous claims concerning this subject matter.

> *The fountain of youth is bottled within the internal wellspring of one youthful thoughts…...it is literally flowing in abundance…waiting for those who desire to drink freely.*

Be that as it may, irrespective of what you have heard, I am here to tell you that I have located this mysterious fountain. I am a well-traveled individual and I have been to many exotic locations worldwide. If you have been in search of it, I have great news. Look no further. I have found it. I will tell you where it is. Are you ready? Here it is. The fountain of youth is bottled within the internal wellspring of one's youthful thoughts. That's right! Everybody is looking outside of themselves for it when it is literally flowing in abundance between their ears and is waiting for those who desire it to drink of it freely.

Jesus said the kingdom or the "KINGDOME" (THE ARENA OF YOUR THOUGHTS) of Heaven is within. This is an interesting thought, a side note if you will, I do not think that people age in Heaven…Hmmm! Interesting! I am certainly not suggesting that this is all to the kingdom of Heaven. One can write 10 million books on this topic and not even begin to scratch the surface concerning this celestial eternal kingdom. I do firmly believe; however, that when Jesus made this statement, He was at least making some reference to ones thinking center.

Thoughts control everything. Youthful thoughts, if persisted in will always result in a youthful appearance and youthful energy. Thoughts of growing old will bring on old age long before its appointed time. We have all seen the forty year old person that looks as they are sixty and vice versa. Some might argue that genes play a major factor here, but I will venture to say genes have little to do with one's youthful appearance. That individual's youthfulness was spawned in the gene pool of their youthful thoughts and what you see is the manifestation and the results of those thoughts. Thoughts cannot be permanently hidden. Your inner thoughts are mere delayed results of your external circumstances.

Remember, thoughts are seeds and most of those seeds will germinate, take root, and produce an external harvest. Thoughts control your destiny. If you really think about it, it is thoughts that give people nervous breakdowns. Thoughts create sickness in the body. Thoughts bring on premature death. Now if this is true, the inverse of this has to be true. It is thoughts that promote emotional health, Thoughts that bring health back to the body, Thoughts that create life. We all must decide on which side of thought we will reside.

People who constantly seem to live their lives in the dungeons of misfortune are not born under some unlucky star; neither are people who seem to live charm lives born under a lucky star. We all either know or have known both types. If it were possible for you to go back and closely trace the thoughts of these people, you will find that those individuals who are the perpetual dungeon dwellers nurtured the thoughts that landed them there and vice versa. One's future circumstances are very predictable. Predicting a person's outcome is no magic by any stretch. It is simply law in action. Psalms chapter 119 in the Holy Bible speaks in depth with reference to law and it would be wise if you were to read it at some point.

Everything that exists today was a thought at one time in a person's mind. Nothing that you see in our world just evolved. Take yourself for example, you were a thought in your parents mind before you were even conceived. This book that you are reading right now was a thought in my mind long before it was ever written (to long I might add). The house or the apartment that you live in was a thought in the architects mind before it took shape. On a more grandiose scale, planet Earth was a thought in the mind of God our Father Creator before it came into being.

Every one of your actions was a prior thought. Your brain (which produces thoughts) is as the central processing unit of a computer. Some CPU'S can perform over 3 billion tasks per second without error. That is pretty amazing. Guess what? The brain created the computer. That means that it is more powerful than any computer.

It is the mind (the subconscious) that tells the heart to beat. It regulates the blood pressure; it makes the pupils of your eyes to dilate when necessary. It allows you to walk, talk, think, and reason. It relays to the lungs how much air is necessary for the body to function properly. The mind is measureless. Studies show that the average person only uses about 10 percent of his or her minds capacity.

When we were fashioned by the Creator in His image and in His likeness, and He gave us this resource that no adjective can describe, He wanted us to understand its capacities and we can only do that if we are in communication and in right standing with Him. This is where faith comes in. We were created to be in partnership with our Creator that is why maintaining a relationship with Him is vital beyond words.

CONCLUSION

King David was by far the greatest king that Israel ever had. He also wrote the book of psalms. What made king David the greatest king to ever sit on the throne was his understanding and execution of spiritual law. Listen to what he states in Psalms 1:3

1 Blessed is the man that walketh not in the council of the ungodly, nor standeth in the way of sinners, nor sitteth in the seat of the scornful.

2 **But his delight is in the law of the Lord; and in his law doth he meditate day and night.**

3 And he shall be like a tree planted by the rivers of water, that bringeth forth his fruit in his season; his leaf also shall not wither; **and whatsoever he doeth shall prosper.** Notice how that he makes reference to the law of sowing and reaping in verse three. David is the only king in the Holy Scriptures that was given the title "A MAN AFTER GOD'S OWN HEART." David from an early age understood the natural and spiritual veracity of these laws and he used them throughout the course of his life. It has been said that Kings and nations would tremble when they heard that David and his army was coming against them. This is just one example of a man who used spiritual law to accomplish many miraculous things. Time would not permit me to go throughout the annals of history to point out numerous others who had an understanding of the reality of God's law.

My hope is you will mentally consume these timeless laws and savor the sweetness of these truths; understanding that all eternal laws are cut from the very loincloth of the Almighty, with his pledge of declaration on them. These immutable inhabitants of eternity have no beginning or no ending. They cannot fail. One will only find great peace, hope, and comfort in the assurance of their accuracy. It is when we surrender our earthly intelligence to their heavenly sapience, that we will only begin our earthly journey on the path to true wisdom, life and blessings both in this life and in the life to come.

A FINAL WORD FROM THE AUTHOR

What you have just read has been tried, practiced and proven over the centuries. This is not a personal philosophy. I am not a philosopher. (Those that know me will fully attest to that). Neither am I a religious teacher because what you just read has nothing to do with religion. Spiritual law and religion are as opposite as day and night.

What I am is a servant; and I am a messenger who is fulfilling his God given assignment here in the Earth realm; and in preparation for the next life. The message you just read is a timeless message. It was written to address and to speak to the timeless sector of your make up; that being your soul. One day your soul will separate itself from your body and will render your body lifeless. This is what we call in this life; death. In the next life however, it is called eternal life because it is at this period that your eternal soul will meet its destiny. This is where philosophy and religion can become very dangerous.

There are many religions in this world; there are just as many philosophies. All of them offer speculation as to what becomes of the soul at the time of death. Jesus Christ said, "Ye shall know the truth, and the truth shall make you free" (John 8:32). According to the Holy Scriptures (The same scriptures that I extracted these laws from) this is what happens.

When the soul separates from the body, a mandate is given to that soul to dwell in one of two destinations. The destinations that I speak about here are Heaven and Hell. This has to be true because according to law and principle, in order for life to exist, there has to be balance. In essence, what I am saying is everything must have an opposite. If we have twelve hours of day, then we must have twelve hours of night. If there is a right way, than there must be a wrong way. If there is a Creator, then there has to be a destroyer. If there are angels from Heaven, then there has to be demons from Hell. If there is the way of truth that leads to freedom and eternal life, then there has to be a way of error that ends in bondage and eternal death.

Jesus Christ said it this way, "Broad *is* the way that leads to destruction and many there be that go there at. But narrow is the way that leads to life and few there be that find it" (Matthew 7:13).

According to the Holy Scriptures, in order for ones soul to enter into the kingdom of Heaven, that soul and spirit must be born again, John 3:7. Contrary to popular belief, everybody does not go to Heaven when they die. According to the Holy Bible, the only ones that make it into the kingdom of Heaven are the individuals who have (in this life) accepted the provision of the gracious gift of salvation by God the Father Creator through his Son Jesus Christ.

Ephesians 2:4-10 states, "*4* But God, who is rich in mercy, for his great love wherewith he loved us,

5 Even when we were dead in sins, hath quickened us together with Christ, (by grace ye are saved;)
6 And hath raised *us* up together, and made us sit together in heavenly *places* in Christ Jesus:
7 That in the ages to come he might shew the exceeding riches of his grace in *his* kindness toward us through Christ Jesus.
8 For by grace are ye saved through faith; and that not of yourselves: it is the gift of God:
9 Not of works, lest any man should boast.

10 For we are his workmanship, created in Christ Jesus unto good works, which God hath before ordained that we should walk in them" KJV.

Just like the body of a child is washed and cleansed in the water of the womb of its mother before its physical entrance into this temporary earthly kingdom; so, in the same way does the soul and the spirit have to be washed and cleansed in the blood of Jesus Christ before its entrance into the spiritual everlasting Heavenly Kingdom.

In talking to Nicodemus Jesus Christ in John 3:3-8 illustrated it this way. *3* Jesus answered and said unto him, Verily, verily, I say unto thee, Except a man be born again, he cannot see the kingdom of God.
4 Nicodemus saith unto him, How can a man be born when he is old? can he enter the second time into his mother's womb, and be born?

5 Jesus answered, Verily, verily, I say unto thee, Except a man be born of water and of the Spirit, he cannot enter into the kingdom of God.

6 That which is born of the flesh is flesh; and that which is born of the Spirit is spirit;

7 Marvel not that I said unto thee, Ye must be born again.

8 The wind bloweth where it listeth , and thou hearest the sound thereof, but canst not tell whence it cometh, and whither it goeth: so is everyone that is born of the Spirit" KJV.

Here is what I am saying in a nutshell. In order for a person to be assured that their soul will go to Heaven when it departs from the body, that person must commit their soul to Jesus Christ and receive the gift of salvation that was provided by God the Father Creator though his Son (Jesus Christ) shed blood on the cross. Jesus stated in John 14:6 "…I am the way, the Truth, and the life: no man cometh unto the Father, but by me."

You may ask how do I receive this gift? Romans 10: 9-13 states,

9 That if thou shalt confess with thy mouth the Lord Jesus, and shalt believe in thine heart that God hath raised him from the dead, thou shalt be saved.

10 For with the heart man believeth unto righteousness; and with the mouth confession is made unto salvation.

11 For the scripture saith, Whosoever believeth on him shall not be ashamed.

12 For there is no difference between the Jew and the Greek: for the same Lord over all is rich unto all that call upon him.
13 For whosoever shall call upon the name of the Lord shall be saved" KJV.

It is very simple. You must pray in faith and ask Jesus to come into your heart and life and to redeem your soul from sin and death. If you are at a loss for words, you can say these words. Dear Heavenly Father my Creator, I pray this in the name of Jesus Christ your Son. I thank you for this gift of salvation that you have provided for me. I confess all my sins to you, and I am asking you to save my soul from sin and eternal damnation. Come into my life and show me what my earthly assignment is, in your Son Jesus Christ's name do I pray, Amen.

GODS BLESSINGS,

GLEN A. NICHOLS

Notes

Notes

Notes

www.ingramcontent.com/pod-product-compliance
Lightning Source LLC
LaVergne TN
LVHW021526080426
835509LV00018B/2677